Socialism or Extinction

Socialism or Extinction:
The meaning of revolution in a time of ecological disaster

Martin Empson

Socialism or Extinction:
The meaning of revolution in
a time of ecological disaster

Martin Empson

First edition published by Bookmarks in 2022

c/o 1 Bloomsbury Street, London WC1B 3QE
www.bookmarksbookshop.co.uk

ISBN 978-1-914143-61-8 paperback
ISBN 978-1-914143-62-5 Kindle
ISBN 978-1-914143-63-2 epub
ISBN 978-1-914143-64-9 pdf

Typeset by Colm Bryce & Kev Kiernan for Bookmarks Publications
Cover design by Roger Huddle
Printed by Halstan & Co, Amersham, England

About the author

Martin Empson is the author of several books and pamphlets including *Land and Labour: Marxism, Ecology and Human History* and *'Kill all the Gentlemen': Class Struggle and Change in the English Countryside.* He also edited *System Change not Climate Change—A Revolutionary Response to Climate Change.* He is a longstanding environmental and socialist activist and a member of the SWP.

Acknowledgements

This book is a polemical intervention into the debates that are happening inside the environmental movement. The arguments in it reflect countless discussions I have had in the environmental and climate movements over 25 years. Most of all, it has been shaped by years of conversations with my comrades in the socialist movement. I dedicate this book to everyone who continues to fight against capitalism's environmental destruction.

I would particularly like to thank several comrades for their comments on early drafts and chapters of this book, all of whom helped make it a far better work. My thanks to Anne Alexander, Alex Callinicos, Charlie Kimber, Amy Leather and Camilla Royle. I owe a debt to all of them, but any errors in the final text are mine. Thanks also to Colm Bryce, Kev Kiernan, Sandra Shepherd and Roger Huddle for their work turning the draft into a final text. My special thanks to Sarah Ensor whose support and encouragement made it possible.

Contents

Introduction

In November 2021, the 26th United Nations Conference of the Parties (COP) climate conference took place in Glasgow. It brought together the signatory nations to the UN's Framework Convention on Climate Change (UNFCCC), just as previous conferences had done almost every year since 1995. The only exception to this conference timeline had been 2020 when Covid postponed COP26 to the following year. Some politicians billed COP26 as the "last chance" for the world to deal with the climate crisis, the rhetoric undermined by similar claims made by their predecessors at earlier COPs. However, just like those earlier conferences, the Glasgow COP was a failure.

Thousands of delegates arrived in Glasgow from around the world. Some 503 of them were representatives of fossil fuel corporations, many attending as members of national delegations. The presence of lobbyists for the coal, oil and gas multinationals was no doubt part of the reason behind COP26's failure—after all, the fossil fuel industry has a long track record of derailing action on climate change. However, the failure in Glasgow was not down to these lobbyists—it arose out of the impossible task that the UN has given to COP. For nearly a quarter of a century COP conferences have tried to solve the climate crisis within the framework of capitalism. But capitalism is the root cause of the climate disaster.

This book will argue that capitalism has unleashed an environmental crisis it cannot solve. Through its very nature, capitalism drives ecological destruction and, simultaneously, erects barriers that prevent us from stopping that crisis. Building a sustainable future will require the end of capitalism and the creation of a new, socialist, world. Understanding capitalism's environmental crisis requires anti-capitalist politics and, because the only conclusion of this can be that capitalism must go, the struggle for a sustainable world needs revolutionary politics. In this book, I will outline the sort of politics we need, and argue that revolution is not an abstract concept from history—but an "actuality" for the 21st century. Indeed revolution is the only hope for humanity's long-term future.

The climate crisis poses big questions, but sometimes the answers seem remarkably straightforward. If burning coal and oil releases carbon dioxide, why do we not invest in renewable energy? Could we use some of capitalism's enormous wealth—perhaps by taxing the billionaires—to fund the infrastructure to reduce emissions? Why is there money for war, but nothing for flood defences in the global south? Why don't rich countries whose economic development has primarily caused the crisis, support the poor countries who suffer most from it? Why don't we plan our economy to meet the needs of people and the planet, instead of in the interest of profit? This book seeks to answer those questions.

*

The failure at COP26 appalled many in the scientific community. In December 2021, the prestigious science journal *Nature*, in an editorial entitled *Sustainability at the Crossroads*, concluded:

> Even if the pledges announced [at COP26] are implemented, temperatures are still projected to rise to a catastrophic 2.4°C by 2100. And below the surface lay disagreements on definitions and the detail of implementation… 'net zero' is one example. There is no agreed definition or measure of it, and without this, it's impossible to know whether pledges will actually

> stop global warming. There is also no agreed definition of climate finance for LMICs (low and middle-income countries). This means that richer countries can make up their quotas with loans or official development aid that links to climate change only indirectly. Arguments have persisted for years over the funding promised more than a decade ago—what has been disbursed and who owes what—and this has undermined trust and has cast a shadow over negotiations, including those in the lead-up to the Glasgow meeting.[1]

Scientists warn that we have to avoid 1.5 degrees of warming above pre-industrial levels. Yet as I write this, the world is already at 1.1 degrees warming and getting closer to the 1.5 degree point. In May 2022, scientists warned that the Earth had a 48 percent chance of hitting 1.5 degrees warming by 2026.[2] This would mean missing the most ambitious global deal on climate change—the Paris Agreement signed in 2015. For years, the UN COP process had used 2 degrees warming as its target. In Paris the countries most immediately impacted by warming, especially the small island states, argued that 1.5 degrees warming was a better target, otherwise sea level rises would destroy them. The adoption of 1.5 degrees was a small victory for countries in the Global South and the environmental movement, which was demanding tougher action.

Stopping climate change before it reaches 1.5 degrees would make a massive difference: sea level rises would be much lower, millions of people would avoid inundation in floods, many species might survive and other significant ecological impacts could be prevented. Even with 1.5 degrees of warming, the impacts would still be enormous, yet meeting this target would avoid far worse impacts. Yet the reality is that without significant action the world is likely on course for much higher levels of warming. The reason for this is the failure of a global environmental strategy that fails to deal with the root cause of the environmental problem—capitalism.

The solutions on offer in Glasgow did not challenge the central tenets of the capitalist system. Capitalism is an economic system fuelled by coal, oil and gas that causes the systematic degradation of nature through its drive to make profits. Rarely is such a critique of capitalism's ecological destruction heard in the COP conference halls or in the mainstream media. Yet millions of people recognise that this system is to blame. During COP26 and despite the limitations imposed by the coronavirus pandemic, hundreds of thousands of people took to the streets to demand real action on climate change.

Tens of thousands of people protested outside the conference hall in Glasgow, and in towns and cities the length and breadth of Britain. In Glasgow around 150,000 demonstrated demanding climate justice. Many of those protesters identified capitalism as the problem carrying placards demanding, "System Change not Climate Change". For revolutionary socialists and anti-capitalists such slogans are encouraging, but they beg a question—what does system change mean?

The answer is not obvious. System change means different things to different activists. For some activists, system change means challenging the worst excesses of capitalist society. This might mean demanding a windfall tax on the profits of fossil fuel corporations or nationalising specific industries to encourage them to work in a more equitable way. There are similarities with sections of the "anti-globalisation movement" which in the early 2000s raised demands for the regulation, and taxation, of financial markets.[3]

Frequently these activists see capitalism as having entered a new era in the 1980s, when the neoliberal policies driven by politicians like US President Ronald Reagan or Britain's Prime Minister Margaret Thatcher led to massive privatisation and deregulation.[4] The institutions created out of these policies, such as the IMF, World Bank or the UNFCCC see their remit through the lens of the free market.

The opening up of every area of society to the free market has made the environmental crisis worse, at the same time as making it harder for society to respond. The standard global response to the climate crisis, the one on display at COP26 and the one that runs through the previous quarter of a century of international attempts to deal with climate change, is one that sees the free market as the only solution. Hence the emphasis from world leaders on carbon trading schemes, the commodification of nature through "Natural Capital", and net zero offsetting plans.[5] So activists like Naomi Klein are right to demand the rolling back of neoliberal, free market policies. As she wrote in her 2019 book, *On Fire*:

> Responding to climate change requires that we break every rule in the free market playbook and that we do so with great urgency. We will need to rebuild the public sphere, reverse privatisations, relocalise large parts of economies, scale back overconsumption, bring back long-term planning, heavily regulate and tax corporations, maybe even nationalise some of them, cut military spending, and recognize our debts to the Global South... none of this has a +hope in hell of happening unless it is accompanied by a massive, broad-based effort to radically reduce the influence that corporations have over the political process.[6]

There is nothing objectionable in any of Klein's demands here. As she says they "supercharge the pre-existing case for virtually every progressive demand". But, they fall short of dismantling the structures of capitalism that have driven environmental destruction since long before the neoliberal era

For other activists system change means the election of progressive politicians who would introduce radical policies such as a Green New Deal. Recently this approach has been most associated with the movements around Jeremy Corbyn in Britain or Bernie Sanders in the United States. No activist would oppose the election of radical politicians whose policies advocate massive economic shifts for a just transition toward a more sustainable economy. However, these plans essentially leave capitalism's structures intact. Which is why Alex Callinicos dubbed earlier manifestations of this type of politics "reformist anti-capitalism".[7] For many the idea of "system change" means a mix of radical demands, electoral projects, local organisation and other ideas. For Marxists the slogan has a specific meaning—the fundamental transformation in the way society is organised. This means revolution.

The word revolution can bring to mind all sorts of different events and meanings. It might evoke the French Revolution, which saw the execution of Louis XVI and Queen Marie Antoinette. It could make you think of the Russian Revolution. More recently, readers might remember the revolutions of the Arab Spring, which saw the fall of governments and dictators throughout the region including, most spectacularly, the fall of Egyptian dictator Hosni Mubarak after nearly 30 years.

We are told that revolutions are bloody affairs that end in violence or dictatorship, and so any attempts to transform society are doomed to failure. Those who argue this often have an interest in defending the status quo. We are also told that revolutions are unusual, and (again usually by apologists for existing regimes) that they are interruptions in the otherwise seamless continuity of capitalist development. In fact, revolutions are remarkably frequent.

In 2007, the British Marxist Chris Harman described the 20th century as a century of revolution. To prove his point he listed revolutions in "Turkey in 1908; revolutions in Russia in 1905 and 1917; the Irish rebellion of 1916-21; the German and Austrian revolutions that overthrew their respective emperors in 1918-19; and the Spanish revolutions of 1931 and 1936". Harman continued by listing uprisings or revolutions in East German (1953), France (1968), Portugal (1974), Poland (1980) and the Eastern European revolutions of 1989-1990. He concluded, "Britain is virtually alone among European states in not having fairly recent memories of revolutionary change... and most of the non-western governments represented at the

UN would not have a seat without the revolutionary movements that ended colonial domination".[8]

The 21st century has also seen mass uprisings. The Arab Spring, the wave of rebellion that swept the Middle East from 2010 to 2011, bringing down politicians, governments and tyrants in countries as diverse as Egypt, Tunisia, Syria, Yemen, Libya, Sudan and many others has already been mentioned. Since then periodic renewals of mass protests have occurred, including what Joseph Choonara has called a "third cycle of struggle" in 2019, which saw revolts in countries like Lebanon, Egypt, Haiti, Iraq and Algeria. Choonara argued that the revolts showed the "growth and vitality of the global working class" which now made up 1.8 billion people.[9]

Capitalism is a system that generates vast wealth, concentrated in the hands of a tiny minority of billionaires, while millions of people suffer from poverty, hunger, malnutrition and unemployment. It drives ecological disaster, threatening the lives of billions of people—according to the United Nations' Intergovernmental Panel on Climate Change, up to 3.6 billion people are already "highly vulnerable" to climate change.[10]

At the same time as driving environmental disaster, capitalism also drives conflict and war. Inherent to its economic system is the competition between rival blocks of capital. On an international level this means competition between nation-states. As I write this, Russia's invasion of Ukraine and the threat of Nato escalation have made global nuclear war a real possibility.

Socialists want to see a world where everyone has a decent life, home, diet, healthcare and education. We also want a planet where biodiversity is protected, where industrial agriculture does not encourage the evolution of new diseases and where society exists within the framework of sustainable global environmental boundaries. In 1915 the Polish-German revolutionary Rosa Luxemburg published an anti-war polemic, the *Junius Pamphlet*. She examined how imperialist competition caused the appalling slaughter in the trenches of the First World

War. Famously she concluded that the choice facing humanity was "socialism or barbarism".[11] Today war and environmental crisis means that barbarism already exists for billions of people. The choice now is between socialism and extinction. That means we need to make "system change" real, by building a revolutionary movement that can overthrow capitalism.

This book is an unapologetic defence of revolution. In it, I explain what Marxists mean by revolution, and defend the concept from those who argue it is impossible, or would be too violent or would inevitably lead to dictatorship. I argue that revolution is not about top-down change, rather it is about ordinary people—the vast majority of the world's population—enacting change from below, and creating a world of genuine, mass, participatory democracy. This means revolution is about workers power—using the strength and organisation of the working class to defeat capitalism and create a socialist society. Crucially revolution means the working class seizing the "means of production"—the factories, industry, land and infrastructure—from the capitalists. Once the working class has control of the means of production, they can organise production in the collective interests of the majority of society and govern our relationship with nature in a sustainable way.

I also argue that if socialists fail in this task, society will not just carry on as before. Aging capitalism offers us no benign future—it presents us with environmental disaster, economic crisis and military violence. If we do not transform the world, the future for humanity is very bleak indeed.

Chapter 1
How capitalism is destroying the world

Capitalism is driving an ecological disaster on an almost incomprehensible scale. This chapter, will look at how climate change is affecting our world, and how capitalism makes this worse. In particular, we will look at how capitalism's divisions such as class, race and gender, push the impact of climate change onto those communities least able to protect themselves.

In August 2021, the United Nations' Intergovernmental Panel on Climate Change (IPCC) published its Sixth Assessment report. In nearly 4,000 pages, it detailed the scale of the crisis humanity faces.

Introducing the report, United Nations secretary general António Guterres said it was "a code red for humanity". It conclusively showed that "human activity" is warming the atmosphere, oceans and land. This warming is associated with unprecedented sea level rises, rainfall levels, increased numbers and intensity of storms, hurricanes and wildfires, droughts and changes in weather patterns.

The IPCC report came out as huge wildfires raged across large areas of Greece and Turkey. These fires forced the evacuation of thousands of people, though their prominence in news reports perhaps reflected their impact on tourist areas. Less public was the way the European Union's neoliberal policies that have cut firefighting services in the name of austerity made these disasters worse.

Climate disaster is a global phenomenon. The development of capitalism enriched the Global North at the cost of the Global South, which has left the countries of the global south more vulnerable to climate disaster.

One of the strengths of the environmental movement during COP26 was the way it placed "climate justice" at the heart of its mobilisation, demanding that the richer nations pay restitution for the destruction they have caused and support sustainable development in the global south.

Also in August 2021, fires in North America destroyed whole towns. The US's National Interagency Fire Centre reported on 8 August 2021, "39,267 wildfires across the country that had burned over 3.5 million acres [1.4 million hectares]". The centre noted that historically the United States and Canada share firefighting resources, but that this year this had proved impossible as both countries were fighting too many fires. Both Mexico and Australia were loaning crew and equipment to Canada.[12]

It was not just in North America and Europe that fires were burning on such a scale. In Siberia, fires consumed 1.5 million hectares. One villager told the *Guardian* "everything is on fire".[13] 2021 also saw major fires in India and Pakistan, Algeria, South Africa, Argentina and many other places.

In June 2021 in Canada's British Columbia province, a "heat dome", which occurs when warm air is trapped above land, led to the deadliest weather event in Canadian history, leading to the death of 525 Canadians.[14] In April 2022 another heat dome over India led to the deaths of thousands of people. In all these examples, it was the poorest people who suffered worst.

At the end of 2021, in what she called a "catastrophic" year, journalist Gabrielle Canon wrote in the *Guardian* that the fire season was longer and explained that megablazes (fires of over 100,000 acres) were "becoming the norm". Canon reported the cost of fighting these fires was $4.4 billion.[15] In February 2022, the UN warned wildfires could be expected in every continent:

> Fire is changing because we are changing the conditions in which it occurs... However, wildfires that burn for weeks and that may affect millions of people over thousands of square kilometres present a challenge that, right now, we are not prepared for... anthropogenic climate change, land-use change, and poor land and forest management mean wildfires are more often encountering the fuel and weather conditions conducive to becoming destructive. Wildfires are burning longer and hotter in places they have always occurred, and are flaring up in unexpected places too, in drying peatlands and on thawing permafrost.[16]

In all of the areas that suffered heatwaves, drought and fires, the human cost was huge. Media reports of such fires tend to focus on immediate destruction and death, with longer term impacts going unreported in the mainstream media. A UN case study of Indonesia reported that fires have increased since the 1980s due to drainage of peatland, expansion of palm-oil agriculture and forest degradation. In 2015 major fires in Indonesia cost the country $16 billion USD, nearly 2 percent of GDP. Nineteen people died from smoke inhalation, but a further 500,000 suffered respiratory illness with "immediate" health-care costs of $151 million USD. Some 5 million children also missed some education as schools closed.[17]

In the Amazon, smoke from deforestation is responsible for the early deaths of 3,000 people every year. [18] There are also further environmental impacts. Many forests are integral parts of wider ecological systems. Their destruction can affect water security, change weather patterns and destroy ecosystems; and fires release carbon dioxide, which causes further global warming and in turn, more fires.

Unequal impacts

The 2021 wildfires were emblematic of the social and ecological crisis that climate change is driving. A warming world drives environmental disruption, raising sea levels, increasing the numbers and intensity of storms and hurricanes, driving drought and fires. Because capitalism is an unequal system, such disasters disproportionately hit poor and oppressed groups. As the United Nations acknowledges:

> Disasters tend to hit the poorest and most marginalised demographics the hardest. Women and girls are particularly exposed to climate-related disaster risk—they are likely to suffer higher rates of mortality, morbidity and economic damage to their livelihoods.[19]

UN figures show that in the 2003 European heatwave more women died than men and "women accounted for 61 percent of fatalities caused by Cyclone Nargis in Myanmar in 2008, 70–80 percent in the 2004 Indian Ocean tsunami, and 91 percent in the 1991 cyclone in Bangladesh".[20]

A 2022 IPCC report noted that while climate change was affecting every part of the world, it was hitting some areas worse particularly "locations with poverty, governance challenges and limited access to basic services and resources, violent conflict and high levels of climate-sensitive livelihoods (e.g., smallholder farmers, pastoralists, fishing communities)". Between 2010 and 2020, these areas had already seen a 15-fold increase in deaths when compared to areas of low vulnerability. Injustices "linked to gender, ethnicity, low income or combinations thereof" made environmental disaster worse.[21]

Victims of environmental disasters, or pollution, are also more likely to be black or Asian. In part this is a result of the historic development of capitalism. But it is also because black and Asian communities are more likely to be sited in areas of vulnerability to environmental disaster and are more likely to be chosen as areas for polluting industry. After Hurricane Katrina hit New Orleans in 2005, over 1,800 people died. In Orleans Parish, where most fatalities occurred, mortality for those over 18 was 1.7 to 4 times higher for black people compared to white people.[22] In the United States, you are more likely to be at risk of health effects from pollution if you are black, Asian, Native American or Hispanic than if you are white. The 2021 *State of the Air* study, an annual report published by the American Lung Association (ALA), looked at who pollution affects in the USA. It concluded that:

> Almost 70 million people of color live in counties that received at least one failing grade for ozone and/or particle pollution. Nearly 14 million people of color live in counties that received failing grades on all three measures, including 9.7 million Hispanics.
>
> It continued:
>
> More than 15.8 million people with incomes meeting the federal poverty definition live in counties that received an F for at least one pollutant. Nearly 2.8 million people in poverty live in counties failing all three measures.

Racism and poverty have made it easier to locate polluting industries, landfills and busy roads in areas where populations are black, Asian or Hispanic. [23] People in these communities are more likely to have conditions, such as asthma, that make them vulnerable to pollution when compared to white people. The ALA adds:

> There is evidence that having low income or living in lower income areas puts people at increased risk from air pollution, although the correlation is not as strong as with race and ethnicity.

Elsewhere we see the same pattern. A study of California wildfires from 2000 to 2020 showed that fires were more common in less economically advantaged areas.[24] You are more likely to be a victim of environmental disaster if you are poor, and this takes place across the world.

The historic development of capitalism has seen emissions of greenhouse gases concentrated from a small number of wealthy countries. However the impact of the warming those gases have caused is worse for less well-off countries, especially the ones that have contributed the least to the problem.

A recent scientific study concluded that nations in the Global South will suffer more, and worse, economic harm from a warming world, when compared to richer countries. [25] Back in 2007, Rajendra Pachauri, the former chair of the IPCC predicted exactly this when he said "It's the poorest of the poor in the world, and this includes poor people even in prosperous societies, who are going to be the worst hit".[26]

Global inequality and "climate debt"

The unequal distribution of wealth between the North and South is a result of the historic development of capitalism. Colonialism and imperialism saw, and continue to see, the massive redistribution of wealth and natural resources from the Global South to the North. The slave trade also saw millions of people forcibly moved from Africa to the Americas. The blood and sweat of slave labour fuelled the rise of capitalism in countries like Britain and the United States. Because of this massive redistribution of wealth, countries in the Global South are unable to afford to develop their own countries in the face of growing environmental disaster. They face the brunt of the climate crisis, but are worst placed to protect their populations.

Looking at historical carbon emissions, it can easily be seen that only a small number of countries are responsible for getting the world to one degree of warming. The vast bulk of cumulative emissions have come from the UK, the USA and European countries. Just six countries—the US, Russia, Germany, Britain, Japan and Canada with just ten percent of the global population, are responsible for 39 percent of cumulative emissions between them.[27] The industrialisation of the Global

North has driven climate change so far—and these countries should be responsible for solving the crisis and its impact.

Britain's colonial expansion brought huge areas of the world under its control. The slave trade helped make Britain the richest power in the world. British capitalism also needed raw materials, sucking in natural resources such as cotton, gold, coal, wood, fish and animal furs from around the globe. British economic development required the destruction of indigenous communities, African societies and global ecology. This is in part why Britain is responsible for around 4.7 percent of historic emissions. These emissions now make a significant contribution to the environmental crisis, which is predominately hitting the Global South.

Other countries have also grown rich through the impoverishment of the rest of the world. The US is responsible for 25 percent of historic emissions, with the 28 countries of the EU responsible for 22 percent. Because emissions are cumulative, this means that Europe and North America are primarily responsible for global warming so far. Some politicians like to blame countries like China and India that are newly industrialising. While it is true that China is responsible for about 13 percent of historic emissions, most of those emissions have occurred since the 1950s.[28] China's emissions in part arise because capitalists in countries like Britain have outsourced production there to maximise profits through lower wages. Emissions themselves have effectively been outsourced. Britain is now the "G7's biggest net importer of CO_2 emissions".[29] However China's rush to industrialise and compete with the rest of the world means that it is rapidly developing fossil fuel infrastructure. One of the problems with capitalism is that it traps industrialising countries into the same fossil fuel logic that paved the way for the development of countries in the Global North.

Despite "climate debt" being acknowledged at COP conferences from 2012 onwards, there is little desire to actually pay any money out. Unless this debt is paid, governments in the

Global South will be unable to protect their citizens from the growing climate crisis. While the Copenhagen Accords pledged £100 billion per year to the Global South little of this money has arrived. Worse, instead of paying cash, countries in the Global North have just refinanced debt, or cancelled loans. As of March 2022, the United States owes the UN's Green Climate Fund $2 billion.

Capitalism's global inequality has ensured that the climate crisis is worse in the poorest parts of the world and continues to ensure that the Global South remains trapped by debt and global inequality, unable to respond to the growing climate emergency.

Climate refugees

Climate crisis causes refugees. We know that war and disasters force people to flee their homes though the specific question of environmental refugees is often ignored. The growing climate crisis has already led to movements of millions of people, temporarily or permanently fleeing environmental disaster. It has also forced politicians, activists and international bodies to take the issue more seriously.

According to the Internal Displacement Monitoring Centre, in 2019, there were 13 million people displaced by cyclones, hurricanes, typhoons and other storms. Floods forced 10 million from their homes, 528,500 fled from wildfires and 276,700 from drought.[30] In an important article on migration and climate change Camilla Royle points out that disasters have caused more displacement in recent years than conflict or violence. While volcanoes and earthquakes also cause large numbers of people to flee, Royle explains that these "geophysical disasters" cause fewer displacements of people than environmental ones. Weather related events, she says, are "unnatural disasters" for two reasons, firstly "because dangerous climate change could have been avoided". Secondly, Royle says:

> The effect that ecological breakdown has on people and the response of states is also shaped by the interests

> of capitalism. Indeed, the outcome of any disaster, whether climate-related or not, will be influenced by the type of society in which it takes place. For example, Cyclone Gorky in Bangladesh in 1991 left at least 138,000 people dead. The following year, Hurricane Andrew hit Florida and Louisiana. Despite being a stronger storm, the death count of 65 was much lower. The way in which social forces shape the outcomes of disasters (including the Covid-19 pandemic) has led many to conclude that the degree to which an event such as a storm becomes a disaster depends on how vulnerable the population is; there is no such thing as a "natural" disaster.[31]

As climate change worsens, the number of people fleeing disasters will grow. Exact numbers of climate refugees are difficult to calculate because climate change is often closely linked with other direct drivers of displacement such as floods or drought. The UN Refugee Agency calculates that between 2008 and 2016 on average some 21.5 million people a year "have been forcibly displaced by weather-related sudden onset hazards".[32] These shocking numbers are expected to grow dramatically. A World Bank report in September 2021 calculated that by 2050 some 215 million people could be "internal climate migrants"—almost 3 percent of the projected population. These migrants will be concentrated in the poorest areas of the world with sub-Saharan Africa having the largest number. However, even the World Bank cautions that these figures may be "conservative" because they only look at "slow-onset climate change impacts acting through water availability, crop productivity, and sea-level rise augmented by storm surge" and only consider climate migration *within* countries. In addition, the World Bank study does not include high-income countries, the Middle East and Small Island States.[33]

The people of the latter areas are likely to experience major displacement as a result of climate change—the Middle East from extreme temperatures and island nations as a result of rising sea levels. As far back as 1990 the first UN IPCC report warned that "half a million people in archipelagos and island nations… could be submerged or lose beaches, multi-use habitats, and arable lands, causing severe economic and social disruption".[34]

The number of refugees resulting from climate change is thus likely to be much higher, with one study, from Cornell University in 2017, predicting up to 1.4 billion climate refugees by 2060.[35] The authors of this study, Charles Geisler and Ben Currens, based their calculations on predictions of the number of people living in low-lying coastal zones, almost all of whom would become "climate migrants".[36]

Whatever the exact numbers of those who will be forced to move by climate change, we know from the response to the refugee crisis resulting from the Syrian war that refugees will not be met with a welcome from governments, but racism, indifference and steel barriers. Most climate refugees will come from the Global South. The difference in response to white refugees from war in Ukraine compared to refugees from North Africa and the Middle East gives an idea of how western governments will treat people from the Global South.

In contrast, the environmental movement has linked demands for action on climate change with solidarity with refugees. During 2019 banners, "welcoming refugees" were popular on Extinction Rebellion protests and Climate Strikes. Refugee, migrant and anti-racist organisations were frequent participants during the COP26 protests. Protesters showed solidarity with the Global South, but did not treat people simply as victims. Those who were most at threat from climate change are also part of the solution. As Camilla Royle concludes, the movement must recognise "the agency of refugees themselves, rather than taking a liberal view that treats them as either passive victims or objects of charity. Climate change is a problem to be solved; people moving from one part of the world to another is not".[37]

Biodiversity

Capitalism is driving the destruction of biodiversity on such an unprecedented scale it has been labelled the "Sixth Extinction". The potential loss of millions of plant and animal species is terrible in itself, but it also matters to humans. Every species that disappears is the loss of a link in the ecological web, with potential further impacts on nature. We risk losing plants that might offer cures for diseases, or help prevent food insecurity.

A landmark United Nations' study in 2019 concluded that 1 million of an estimated 8 million species are threatened by extinction. Other figures emphasise the scale of the biodiversity crisis; 500,000 species (9 percent of terrestrial species) have "insufficient habitat for long-term survival".[38]

Natural disasters also damage biodiversity. The Australian bushfires of 2019/2020 killed or injured 3 billion animals according to the World Wildlife Fund. Shocking though these numbers are, the real threat to biodiversity is the way capitalist production degrades the natural world in the interests of profit. To understand this, let us look at food production today.

The diversity of humanity's food source has collapsed in the last century. Historically humans have produced food from around 6,000 different species. Today almost all of the food that humanity eats comes from fewer than 200 species and 66 percent of it comes from just eight plants (sugar cane, maize, rice, wheat, potatoes, soybeans, oil-palm fruit, and cassava).[39]

The reason behind this decline is a food system geared towards maximising profit through industrial production.[40] The development of capitalism is closely associated with the growth of a model of farming that uses high inputs of chemical fertilisers and pesticides, to maximise crop yields and profits. This type of farming also depends heavily on fossil fuels to power machinery. In the Global North, particularly in the United States, a small number of extremely large corporations dominate this type of agriculture and wider food industry.

Following the Second World War, the United States began exporting this agricultural model to the rest of the world. There were two main reasons for this. Firstly, they wanted to create a global food system that would strengthen US capitalism—by providing markets for food staples like beef and wheat—and to make the rest of the world produce export crops for the Global North. In addition, by imposing industrial agriculture on the rest of the world, they could tie farming into a wider industrial system dominated by US multinationals to maximise profits.

In the 1960s and 1970s the US also feared that population growth in the Global South would lead to huge, hungry, rebellious populations. Fear of Communist "Red" revolution saw the US imposing the "Green Revolution" on the Global South. Heavily dependent on technology and chemical inputs, this Green Revolution relied on a small number of high-yield crops, making traditional farming unviable and sidelining many crops.

The Green Revolution did not end hunger. In fact, it made millions of people more vulnerable to hunger and malnutrition. Entire countries went from being food producers to food importers. Traditional agriculture was destroyed and the variety of species farmed collapsed. Agriculture has become reliant on a shrinking number of crop types, with seeds often patented by Western multinationals, which require specific pesticides to farm successfully. Agriculture in the Global South became wedded to economic systems designed to benefit Western capitalism, and millions of peasants and agricultural producers lost their livelihoods. As Timothy Wise explains:

> The peril... was that when foreign capital landed with both feet it was usually on land already occupied and cultivated by farming communities. And the wave of modernization didn't usually carry peasant farmers forward with a rush, it buried them along with their crops and communities.[41]

This agricultural model also destroys biodiversity. Monoculture—the farming of single crops in vast fields—maximises profits because it reduces the amount of labour and machinery needed to plant and harvest. But it also requires heavy usage of pesticides and fertilisers, killing wildlife and plants. The trend towards larger and larger fields destroys hedgerows and spaces that allow wild species to grow and support animal life. In countries like Britain this type of farming has led to a collapse in biodiversity since the Second World War. Its export to the rest of the world is driving a similar process.

The decline in the number of species grown for food and farming models that destroy wider ecosystems is one aspect of the biodiversity crisis caused by industrialised farming. The other is the way that capitalism's push to maximise profits means agriculture is constantly expanding into new areas. One example is the clearance of vast areas of the Amazon rainforest to create agricultural areas for cattle farming or biofuel production.

The biodiversity crisis has not appeared from nowhere in the last few years. Genetic diversity in wild species has decreased by 1 percent per decade since the mid-19th century. [42] But the process has dramatically accelerated in the last 50 years, closely coinciding with the neo-liberal era. The UN argues that the "drivers" of extinction are, in decreasing order of importance, "changes in land and sea use; direct exploitation of organisms; climate change; pollution; and invasion of alien species."

These direct causes arise from "indirect drivers" which, according to the authors of the UN report, derive from "production and consumption patterns, human population dynamics and trends, trade, technological innovations and local through global governance".[43]

Notably, even the UN acknowledges that biodiversity loss is not driven by the behaviour of everyone. In fact, they point out that some communities actually make a positive contribution towards protecting biodiversity and preventing extinction. For instance, the report states that the "lands of Indigenous peoples and local communities, including farmers, pastoralists and herders, are often important areas for in situ conservation of the remaining varieties and breeds".[44]

It is clear that we are living through a major extinction

event. This crisis is associated with the way that capitalism organises production.

We are experiencing an ecological crisis on multiple fronts. As climate change worsens, it will increase the number and intensity of environmental disasters, and in turn, those disasters will fuel further environmental destruction.

While everyone is threatened by this crisis, it is the poor and oppressed in society who suffer first and foremost from environmental disaster. This is because of the nature of capitalism, a society divided by class, racism and gender.

But the ecological crisis is not simply made worse by capitalism. Capitalism causes environmental destruction because of how it organises production. In the next chapter, we will explore this by looking at how capitalism works and how it relates to the natural world.

Chapter 2
How capitalism works

The simplest critique of capitalism is that it causes ecological destruction, poverty, hunger, war and oppression because it puts profit before people and planet. In this chapter, we will explore exactly why it is that happens. In particular, we need to examine the two key divisions in capitalist society—the exploitation of the working class by the capitalist class and the competition between capitalists themselves.

The greatest critic of capitalism was Karl Marx who, together with his friend and collaborator Friedrich Engels, developed a body of work that explored how capitalism functioned, its impact and how it could be overthrown. In their work they developed a deep understanding of how the system caused exploitation, oppression and ecological destruction. Marx and Engels' most famous work is the *Communist Manifesto*, first published in 1848. Many activists are surprised when they first read the *Manifesto* to find the opening chapters begin by appearing to celebrate capitalism:

> The bourgeoisie, during its rule of scarce one hundred years, has created more massive and more colossal productive forces than have all preceding generations together. Subjection of Nature's forces to man, machinery, application of chemistry to industry and agriculture, steam-navigation, railways, electric telegraphs, clearing of whole continents for cultivation,

> canalisation of rivers, whole populations conjured out of the ground—what earlier century had even a presentiment that such productive forces slumbered in the lap of social labour?[45]

Marx and Engels celebrated the dynamism of capitalist production over earlier societies, such as the feudal systems that it replaced in Western Europe. But they quickly went on to caution:

> Modern bourgeois society, with its relations of production, of exchange and of property, a society that has conjured up such gigantic means of production and of exchange, is like the sorcerer who is no longer able to control the powers of the nether world whom he has called up by his spells.

Feudal society had stagnated and become a "fetter" on the further development of society. The overthrow of this old order by the growing capitalist class had ushered in new social relations—capitalist ones—but these in turn had become a "fetter" on the further development of society.

What are capitalist relations and why are they so destructive? Capitalist production is a system of generalised, competitive, commodity production. Each individual firm produces commodities to sell in order to realise profit. They do this within a system where they are in competition with thousands of other producers who are also trying to make a profit.

Capitalist production, like all other historical societies, bases production on two things: human labour and the natural world. Human labour, Marx argued, was the "appropriation of nature for the satisfaction of human needs". All historical societies whether small hunter-gatherer communities, feudal societies or capitalism have an impact upon the natural world. This is firstly because throughout human history we have had to use natural resources such as wood, soil, metal or stone to satisfy our basic needs, and secondly because the by-products of production such as waste and pollution, need to go somewhere.

What changes throughout human history is that the particular way we organise production has differing impacts upon the natural world. While even our distant ancestors may have helped drive certain animals to extinction through hunting, it is only when we reach the capitalist era that systematic, global environmental crisis becomes a reality.

Capitalism is a class system that has smashed humanity's relationship with nature apart. Instead of a relatively sustainable interaction between human society and the natural world, capitalism sees the unrestricted degradation of nature. Capitalist production is predicated on unrestricted growth. In the drive to maximise profits, this growth means nature is used in an unsustainable way.

But capitalism is also a system based on exploitation. As Alex Callinicos has written, it "rests on a profound injustice".[46] Marx put it quite bluntly:

> The capitalist gets rich, not, like the miser, in proportion to his personal labour and restricted consumption, but at the same rate as he squeezes out labour-power from others, and compels the worker to renounce all the enjoyments of life.[47]

Under capitalism workers are compelled to sell their ability to work (their labour power) to a capitalist. Let us imagine a worker employed by a boss for a single day. Each day this worker produces commodities or services which are worth a certain amount of value. The worker is paid a wage in return. However, the worker does not take the whole day to produce value equivalent to their day's wage. It might be that in the course of an eight-hour day, a worker takes two hours to produce commodities of the same value as their wage. During the other six hours, they produce surplus value—which is the source of the bosses' profits. This exploitative relationship between capitalist and worker is unique to capitalism and is at the heart of capitalist production. It means that the capitalist always gets more from the worker, than the worker gets in return. Workers can organise to get a bigger portion of the value they create—by striking for higher wages for instance—but they cannot get rid of exploitation itself without ending capitalism. At the same time for the capitalists to increase their profits they have to squeeze more out of the workers—through cutting wages, or making them work harder and longer.

There is a second key dynamic to capitalist production - the competition between capitalists. Again, this is a unique dynamic to capitalism. In previous class societies, the limit of exploitation by the ruling class was the satisfaction of the needs of their class. Most of the surplus value extracted by the capitalist from their workers is pumped back into the production process to produce further surplus value. There is no limit to this dynamic.

Capitalist production is endlessly hungry. Capitalists take some of the surplus value and reinvest it—as new technology or machinery—to expand production or they might use it to invest in new technology that improves the efficiency of their production, or reduces their labour costs. They might reinvest in technology that creates new products. Why do capitalists behave like this? Why are they constantly reinvesting surplus value and reinventing themselves?

They do this because they are in competition with other capitalists. If an individual capitalist stands still then their rivals will improve efficiency, reduce costs or produce new products and undercut them. The capitalist is compelled to accumulate wealth through a constant process of extracting surplus value and then reinvesting it by the very nature of the capitalist production system. As Marx said, "Accumulate, accumulate! That is Moses and the prophets!... Accumulation for the sake of accumulation, production for the sake of production".[48]

It is worth emphasising two things here. All capitalist production requires the use of natural resources through the exploitation of human labour. Because competitive accumulation is central to capitalist production, there is no limit on the system's degradation of nature. It is the uncontrolled accumulation of wealth, for the sake of further accumulation, that drives capitalism's destruction of nature. Just as capitalism cannot function without exploitation of human labour, it cannot avoid destroying nature in an uncontrolled, irrational, unplanned way.

But workers' are not just victims of exploitation. Their unique position within the capitalist economy gives them enormous strength. Workers' ability to withhold their labour means that they can stop the capitalist accumulation machine—directly hitting the profits of the bosses. Without workers, capitalist accumulation cannot happen. This is why socialists argue that workers' power can destroy capitalism. But workers' power is not just about destruction. In revolutionary struggle, workers' can create their own organisations, which begin to organise society in new ways. Such organisations will form the basis for a socialist society, based on satisfying human need, not competitive accumulation.

Waste and overproduction

Two further aspects of capitalist production are linked to the dynamic of accumulation and have major consequences for the environment. These are waste and overproduction.

Capitalist production is enormously wasteful. Part of that waste arises out of the system's need to use money, resources and human labour on aspects of production that only exist to perpetuate the system itself. The British Marxist, Mike Kidron, calculated that in 1970, "three fifths of the work actually undertaken" produced waste. This included advertising and arms, as well as goods produced for luxury consumption by the rich.[49]

But waste also arises out of the system's inefficiency, which is often related to the nature of production itself. The British food industry, for instance, throws away vast amounts of food. In 2018 9.5 million tonnes of food was wasted, 70 percent of which was intended for consumption—equivalent to 15 billion meals.[50] Campaigns to reduce waste often focus on the consumers who throw uneaten food out at home but this is not the real problem. Most waste in the food system occurs because it is geared towards maximising profits through intensive agriculture and centralised distribution. Supermarkets in particular waste enormous amounts of food because they impose particular conditions on the food supplied by farmers—demanding, for instance, it is a specific shape and colour. According to a 2018 report by the Feedback charity 66 percent of farmers said that retailers caused food waste by over-emphasis on the appearance of food. The National Farmers' Union (NFU) reported that in 2014 a fifth of the Gala apple crop was wasted because it didn't meet the specification that apples had to be fifty percent red. Prices were too low to use the apples elsewhere.[51]

Supermarkets drive over-production of food as farmers hope to have enough qualifying products so they can make a living, or because they are concerned about missing out on sales. Overproduction leads to low prices which means that some crops end up not being worth harvesting and are left to rot. The supermarket model leads to wasted food, primarily because it is driven by their need to maximise profit. Waste arises from a structural problem with the food system.

Other figures show high levels of waste in other parts of the economy. A 2015 report on energy use found that 54 percent of all energy produced in the British is wasted before it reaches homes or businesses, a major cause of this being heat wasted in power stations and inefficient electrical grid infrastructure.[52] We can find other examples across the economy, as companies sacrifice efficiency savings in order to maximise profit.

There is another aspect to capitalism's waste connected to the central dynamic of accumulation. Because capitalists are in competition with each other, there is a tendency towards over-production of commodities. Decisions about what is produced (and in what quantities) are made on the basis of what the capitalists think is going to be profitable. This has nothing to do with satisfying need. The capitalists like to insist that their system is geared toward satisfying human need, but as Marx pointed out it is really about profit:

> In capitalist production what matters is not the immediate use value but the exchange value and, in particular, the expansion of surplus value. This is the driving motive of capitalist production, and it is a pretty conception that—in order to reason away the contradictions of capitalist production—abstracts from its very basis and depicts it as a production aiming at the direct satisfaction of the consumption of the producers.[53]

Because production is not coordinated between manufacturers, they make goods even if there are not enough consumers. The drive to make profit leads to overproduction, which wastes raw materials, labour and energy. If, because there is a glut on the market, these goods cannot be sold then they are scrapped—even if there is a need for them.

Think of the food waste described in the previous section, which takes place at the same time that there are millions of hungry people. Car manufacturers have chronically over-produced cars for decades yet the world cries out for sustainable transport systems. A rational economic system would use the skills and resources of automobile workers to produce buses and light-rail vehicles instead of producing vast numbers of unsaleable cars.

Again, this is an irrationality highlighted by Marx:

> The word overproduction in itself leads to error. So long as the most urgent needs of the large part of society are not satisfied ... there can of course be absolutely no talk of overproduction of products—in the sense that the amount of products is excessive in relation to the need for them. On the contrary, it must be said that

> on the basis of capitalist production there is constant underproduction in this sense. The limits to production are set by the profit of the capitalist and in no way by the needs of the producer. But overproduction of products and overproduction of commodities are two entirely different things.[54]

Over time, economic crisis drives some companies bankrupt, leaving their assets to be bought up by the survivors. As a result, capital becomes concentrated in the hands of smaller and smaller numbers of corporations. Large companies buy out smaller rivals to protect their profits. The concentration of capital like this means that smaller and smaller numbers of companies dominate global production. Just 10 companies produce almost all the food consumed in the world, and a shrinking number of supermarkets distribute it. In Britain just four chains control around 70 percent of grocery sales.

The larger and more powerful corporations can use their economic muscle to destroy emerging rivals. Small rivals are prevented from developing a market share, even if the product they are producing is more efficient, cheaper or better for the environment.[55] We are told that reducing waste and inefficiency in the interests of saving money and the environment lies in our own hands—we need to buy less food, or turn off appliances to save energy. Yet most waste comes from the irrational nature of production, not the choices we make as individuals. Tackling waste means focusing on capital as a system of production, not consumption.

Capitalism and nature

What is "nature"? We might think of the natural world in terms of landscapes, trees, flowers or animals. Capitalism, however, sees nature through the lens of capital accumulation. The natural world is embedded into production, as the system uses it for resources or as a dump for the absorption of pollution. The capitalist sees the natural world as an externality. It does not figure in their calculations and becomes a "free gift" to the capitalist, which is one reason why the system treats the natural world with such disdain.

Marx, following other classical economists, did not see nature as creating surplus value, but it did have a use-value—it could be used for something. The use-value of nature arose from its physical properties - wood could be burnt for heating, fruit can be eaten and so on. So while only human labour could create surplus value, nature was an intrinsic part of the production process. In the opening lines of his work, *The Critique of the Gotha Programme*, Marx polemicised against other socialists:

> Labour is not the source of all wealth. Nature is just as much the source of use-values (and it is surely of such that material wealth consists!) as labour, which itself is only the manifestation of a force of nature, human labour power.

John Bellamy Foster explains the importance of this understanding of the nature-society relationship:

> Both the economic and ecological contradictions of capitalism have their source in the contradictions between the valorization process and the material bases of existence inherent in capitalist commodity production.[56]

For Marx, only human labour could transform the free-gifts of nature into surplus value. In other words, the system cannot function without the labour of the working class, which gives workers, and the working-class, enormous power within capitalist society.[57]

The concept of nature being a "free gift" to the economy is worth looking at in a little more detail. Marx noted how, the development of capitalism transformed the way people understood nature:

> For the first time, nature becomes purely an object for humankind, purely a matter of utility; ceases to be recognised as a power for itself; and the theoretical discovery of its autonomous laws appears merely as a ruse so as to subject it under human needs, whether as an object of consumption or as a means of production.[58]

So capitalism saw nature in terms of its relationship to the capitalist system of production but it also turned it into a commodity itself. We can contrast this with how non-capitalist communities saw and related to nature. On arrival in the Americas, European colonists often looked at the landscape through their frame of reference. They saw the land as ready to be carved up for agriculture, a terra nullius, uninhabited and unused and judged natural resources such as trees or animals in terms of their potential use as a commodity for export—lumber for Europe, or animal skins and furs. This contrasts with indigenous, non-capitalist, societies that saw nature as an ecological system of which they were part.

Many colonists dismissed nature outside of its potential link to capital accumulation. In 1864, W C B Wilson, a surveyor in Queensland, Australia wrote the following illuminating observation of the land he was studying:

> Heavy showers fell which had a wonderful effect upon the hitherto parched up ground innumerable bulbous roots shooting up their long green stems in every direction and clothing the earth with a profusion of flowers.... It is very delightful to contemplate Nature in her holiday garbs, but unfortunately both the flowers and the coarse green grass are intrinsically worthless.[59]

This colonial approach also systematically downplayed, or ignored, the ways in which indigenous people around the world had utilised the landscape in sustainable ways for millennia. As author Bill Gammage notes about Wilson, he "missed seeing that the country had been made", that the labour of generations of Aboriginal people had shaped the landscape to ensure it produced the best possible food for them and their communities. This widely different approach to nature arose from a different social organisation.

European colonialism imposed new social, economic and political relations on the rest of the world. Through disease, violence and slavery it also led to the systematic destruction of indigenous people and their way of life.

John F Richards has written about the way that the interests of European capitalism transformed the ecological and social relations of Native Americans through trade. He writes about how the Native Americans entered into an economic relationship with colonists who encouraged them to hunt animals for skins.

> One after another, Indian ethnic groups drawn into trading furs for goods suffered the fate of all human groups who gain a livelihood by extraction of natural resources for the world economy. In responding to market signals, the Indians necessarily changed their patterns of hunting in order to obtain the specialised products most in demand.[60]

The needs of the market forced Native Americans to transform their relationship to the animals they hunted. Rather than hunt what they needed for survival, they now systematically killed animals in order to satisfy the commercial interests of traders even when species were declining to low levels. Native American hunters themselves became trapped by the logic of the market.

While market relations transformed Native Americans, the greatest destruction came from the settler colonialists. In the mid 19th century there were up to 60 million buffalo on the plains of the United States, but by the end of the century the number had fallen to about 300. The mass killing was part of the genocidal war of the colonialists against the Native American people of the plains who relied on the buffalo for survival.

Everywhere capitalism arrived, it transformed people and nature into its own image tying them both to global markets. [61]

Chapter 3
Can capitalism be greened?

We have seen that capitalism is an inherently destructive system. Because it is based on exploitation as well as the systematic degradation of nature, it is simultaneously anti-human and anti-ecology. Many capitalists understand this. They understand that there is a problem. The UNFCCC and the COP process arose from a recognition by some politicians in the 1980s of the need to address climate change. The creation of the UNFCCC was an explicit attempt to deal with climate crisis within the wider framework of capitalist relations.[62]

Politicians were careful not to imply by this that there had to be a break with how capitalism behaved. Indeed, many economists wanted to embed nature further into the capitalist market. The logic was simple. If you can integrate nature into the market then the market can change nature. One by-product of this would be that some people could also get very rich. Indeed the attraction of these schemes for the capitalist system is that it leaves capitalist production untouched, creating new opportunities for profit while allowing the most polluting of industries to continue their behaviour without restriction.

Economic thinking like this is the origin of the carbon markets and emissions trading schemes that are central to mainstream attempts to reduce emissions. But, it is precisely because the COP process has relied on such free-market mechanisms that the 30 years of COP meetings have achieved nothing.

In the logic of capitalism, turning greenhouse gases into

a commodity that can be bought and sold in a carbon market, is supposed to reduce emissions precisely because capitalists can profit from the transactions. But the buying and selling of "carbon credits"—the right to pollute—leaves wider capitalist relations untouched. It does not lead to the closure of any coal mines or a wider challenge to capitalism's drive to accumulate. The financialisation of nature cannot overcome capitalism's inherently negative ecological impact.

This has not stopped the capitalists trying. During, and in the run up to COP26 the rhetoric around "net zero" was closely associated with offset and trading schemes. The most prominent of these are carbon markets. Such schemes are not new, having been around, in one form or another since the signing of the Kyoto Protocols at a UN summit in 1992. They are supposed to work through a process of assigning "rights to emit" pollutants to individual firms, corporations or countries who can then trade these rights, usually known as carbon credits, on the market. A company that burns fewer fossil fuels than it has credits for can sell its excess credits. The company that buys them can then burn more than its original allocation. Over time, the total number of credits is supposed to be reduced, lowering total emissions.

In reality, such schemes are open to corruption and abuse. A more fundamental problem arises from how companies can create offsetting schemes. For instance, Larry Lohmann, a critic of carbon markets, describes a case where giant industrial pig farms in Mexico, owned by a US multinational, earn "extra revenue by capturing the methane given off by the huge volumes of pig excrement they produce and burning it, and then selling the resulting carbon credits".[63] The generation of credits in this case relies on the fact that methane is a more powerful greenhouse gas than carbon dioxide so by burning it the farms can claim to be reducing levels of warming. As can easily be seen in this case, nothing is actually happening to reduce emissions at all. Some companies even find that they have made more money from selling carbon credits than from their core production. The creation of huge "derivative" financial schemes based on the buying and selling of carbon credits ties these supposedly ecological systems to the whims of the global financial system. In January 2013 the European Emissions Trading Scheme saw the price of carbon fall to a record low. Low prices mean there is little incentive to reduce pollution.

This is the flaw with the seemingly logical idea of "net zero". As the name suggests, making something net zero implies that pollution from a factory, an economic sector or an entire country can be cancelled out by pollution-reducing behaviour elsewhere in the economy. The term however is often misused by politicians and business people to imply zero emissions at the source. In either sense it is greenwashing.

While the process sounds straightforward, in practice offsetting emissions to achieve net zero is extremely difficult. Tree planting is commonly suggested as an example of offsetting, because trees absorb carbon as they grow. But, large scale planting of trees is difficult and can actually cause wider environmental issues. There is a problem of scale and time—offsetting emissions from a single factory might require thousands of trees, which would need to survive for decades to absorb the carbon they are supposed to offset.

Then there is the problem of what happens to the trees. Should the trees be burnt, or die off, then the carbon is released, cancelling out any offsetting. Long after a company has offset some emissions in a quest for net zero the new forest needs to be thriving, and that cannot be guaranteed in a world of increased wildfires. There are even cases when plantations designed to offset emissions in the Global North have seen the displacement of communities in the Global South.

Nonetheless, there are plenty of corporations that will happily claim to have made themselves carbon neutral by planting trees, or investing in some other dubious scheme. Rarely do they give any thought to longer-term consequences. Indeed, offsetting companies themselves are keen to celebrate the profits they make from such dodgy environmental accounting, while glossing over the limitations of their practices.

Patrick Bond gives one examination of how capitalist attempts to offset emissions through carbon markets means that poorer communities suffer in the interests of corporations. In 1980 the Bisasar Road landfill was built on a nature reserve in an Indian neighbourhood of Durban, under apartheid South Africa. The area became a "cancer hotspot" with residents suffering from the stink and developing health problems such as "asthma, sinusitis, pneumonia and even tuberculosis". After years of campaigning the African National Congress (ANC), which led the fight against apartheid, promised that it would close the landfill. But in the 2000s, the ANC government allowed the landfill to continue because they could earn money by selling carbon credits associated with the burning of methane.[64] They continued to ignore the health effects on black and Indian communities in the area in favour of generating profits.

Whole industries have developed around carbon offsetting. Companies will promise to cancel out your personal emissions from a flight, or those produced by factories and industries. While the schemes appear to work like a mathematical equation, with the figures and symbols on one side balancing out those on the other, the reality is much more complex. Indeed, as the IPCC cautions, these schemes can be shown to have made global warming worse:

> Risks arise from some responses that are intended to reduce the risks of climate change, including risks from maladaptation and adverse side effects of some emission reduction and carbon dioxide removal measures (high confidence). Deployment of afforestation of naturally unforested land, or poorly implemented bioenergy, with or without carbon capture and storage, can compound climate-related risks to biodiversity, water and food security, and livelihoods, especially if implemented at large scales, especially in regions with insecure land tenure (high confidence).[65]

Emissions trading schemes, carbon offsetting and the privatisation of nature that they are based on, are the logical consequences of neoliberalism. We should reject them utterly. As Lohmann has said, "Carbon markets are not designed to reduce emissions. Their function... is to extend the life of the fossil fuel economy and, indirectly, an exploitative and unequal system of extractivism and nature degradation. That is why they are backed by so many fossil-driven corporations and capitalist states. Carbon markets have coexisted very happily for more than 20 years with a catastrophic increase in emissions."[66]

Carbon trading and similar market mechanisms have failed to dent growing levels of emissions. These schemes are attractive to the capitalists because they appear to offer a way of dealing with climate change while allowing capitalist production to continue as normal. Instead, they have failed to reduce emissions on any scale at all, and have brought us closer to disaster.

Green New Deals and environmental reforms

The free market is no solution to capitalism's environmental destruction, so what about policies that blunt or try to limit capitalism's excesses? Earlier we saw how some radical activists look to reform capitalism to make it more socially just and less environmentally destructive. One proponent of this strategy is Canadian radical journalist Naomi Klein. As Klein points out:

> The bottom line is that an ecological crisis that has its roots in the overconsumption of natural resources must be addressed not just by improving the efficiency of our economies, but also by reducing the amount of material stuff that the wealthiest 20 percent of people on the planet consume. Yet that idea is anathema to the large corporations that dominate the global economy, which are controlled by footloose investors who demand ever-greater profits year after year.

Klein continues, "The way out is to embrace a managed

transition to another economic paradigm".[67] One of my central arguments in this book is that a "managed transition" out of capitalism is not possible. We will need a revolutionary movement to achieve such radical change. Nonetheless, Klein is right to argue for a "dramatic reining in of the market forces that created and are deepening the crisis". [68] A fight by workers for a Green New Deal can be part of winning important reforms as well as developing the combativity and organisation of the workers' movement. While Green New Deals and other, similar, programmes cannot stop capitalism's environmental destruction, they are part of the fight for wider, systemic change.

In this section, I will look in a little more detail at the "Green New Deal"—acknowledging that the GND has several different models—and compare it with the demand for Climate Jobs, which has come from environmental activists and trade unionists in Britain. Firstly, what is a Green New Deal? Klein explains:

> The idea is a simple one: in the process of transforming the infrastructure of our societies at the speed and scale that scientists have called for, humanity has a once-in-a-century chance to fix an economic model that is failing the majority of people on multiple fronts.[69]

While variations on a Green New Deal have been around for decades, the issue made it into public consciousness in February 2019 when US Democratic Representative Alexandria Ocasio-Cortez and Senator Edward J Markey tabled a resolution for a Green New Deal (GND). Ocasio-Cortez and Markey's GND arose out of the growing radicalism of the US environmental movement. The text of their resolution [70] acknowledged the close links between climate crisis and inequality, poverty and racial injustice in the United States, and called for a "a new national, social, industrial, and economic mobilization on a scale not seen since World War II" to tackle climate crisis and create jobs, prosperity and tackle "systematic injustices".

The plan immediately drew the anger of Republicans and

President Donald Trump who sought to use the GND as a divisive issue in the coming election. The right argued that a GND would cost jobs and was irrelevant to ordinary voters. Unfortunately, a vote in March 2019 saw the GND defeated 57-0 in the US senate.

The inspiration for the Green New Deal comes from the reforms introduced by US President Franklin D Roosevelt in the 1930s. Roosevelt's "New Deal" was an attempt to deal with the economic crisis of the late 1920s and early 1930s by using state funding to support the unemployed and create jobs. This saw the funding of unemployment relief, investment in public works such as road building and financial stimulation for the agricultural sector.

There was more to the New Deal than just creating jobs and helping struggling sectors of the US economy. The radical US historian Howard Zinn points out that the New Deal had two agendas. Firstly it was intended to "reorganise capitalism in such a way to overcome the crisis and stabilise the system" and secondly to "head off the alarming growth of spontaneous rebellion in the early years of the Roosevelt administration—organisation of tenants and the unemployed, movements of self-help, general strikes in several cities".[71]

US capitalism urgently needed this support. The economic crisis was causing impoverishment and discontent on a huge scale. In 1932 unemployment was at 24 percent. Agencies such as the Federal Emergency Relief Administration helped 28 million people (22 percent of the population) by April 1934 turning away a further 7 million. Between 1933 and 1940, the US government spent $16 billion on relief.[72]

Unemployment and poverty on this scale also led to resistance by the working class. A contemporary Marxist, Mauritz Hallgren, noted that there had been "more disturbances and disorders from 1929 to 1933 than in any other comparable period in the history of the country".[73] Socialist historian John Newsinger describes 1934 in the US as the "year of the fightback". Massive strike waves shook the economy. Three strikes in particular, the Electric Auto-Lite strike in Toledo, the

Teamsters in Minneapolis and the San Francisco dockers "were to reach almost insurrectionary proportions and completely change the strategic context for the American working class".[74]

It was in this context that Roosevelt introduced the New Deal. His administration was careful to make minor concessions to workers when their organisation was strong, but where it was not, it supported business interests. The New Deal gave small concessions to those who were most desperate to prevent them from "turning a rebellion into a real revolution". [75]

One section of the US population failed by Roosevelt were black workers, as the New Deal kept segregation and differences in wages and relief between black and white workers in place.

The New Deal remains a touchstone for radicals today seeking inspiration for the fight against 21st century capitalism. Chris Saltmarsh, a British activist with Labour for a Green New Deal argues that a modern GND must learn from both the positives and negatives of the 1930s experience. He writes that:

> The Green New Deal must structure racism out of economic policy, rather than further bake it in as the New Deal did... our lesson from New Deal is that governments are susceptible to pressure from both reactionary forces promoting racial segregation or discrimination or progressive forces like the labour movement.

He continues by stressing that a Green New Deal should "make anti-racism central".[76] Such "socialist" Green New Deals will inspire many who are sick of capitalism's destruction of public services and the environment. Saltmarsh demands, among other things, democratic public ownership of key industries and economic institutions, arguing that the more of the economy that is under public ownership the "more effectively government can centrally plan the energy transition".[77] This radical GND would see fossil fuel companies nationalised and shut down, the creation of "green jobs" in sustainable industries and a series of national services run along the lines of the NHS, in energy, housing, transport and food to manage a transition to a sustainable economy. For Saltmarsh, principles of economic and political justice, encapsulated by "public ownership, green jobs, just transition, universal basic services and global justice" are central to this response to four decades of neoliberalism.[78]

While plans for a GND are often popular, the challenge for their proponents is getting them implemented. When it came to the US election, President Biden did not endorse a GND, instead arguing for a much less ambitious plan. The best GND plans, the ones that have the most far-reaching changes, are also the ones that most challenge the vested interests of fossil fuel corporations and the capitalist system. They immediately face barriers from the right. Donald Trump's comments on the GND were often ridiculous, suggesting that it would force people to have "tiny little windows" or "eliminate all Planes, Cars, Cows, Oil, Gas & the Military". But right-wing rhetoric, that argues a GND, would destroy jobs and the economy must be countered by concrete proposals and mass campaigning.

The British Climate Jobs campaign has sought to do this by linking its proposals directly to the creation of jobs, structured though a National Climate Service organised along the lines of the British National Health Service. Many in the British trade union movement have taken up the proposals and the campaign has spurred several emulations around the world.[79]

This campaign came out of a conference called by the trade union group of the Campaign Against Climate Change. In 2009 the group produced the first edition of the *One Million Climate Jobs* pamphlet. In 2021 the fourth edition was published, called *Climate Jobs: Building a Workforce for the Climate Emergency* which contains expanded plans to transform the economy to avoid the "existential threat of climate breakdown".[80] The campaign emphasises the importance of the "public sector" to delivering these jobs and coordinating the economic strategy. Suzanne Jeffery the editor of the most recent report explains that in the climate jobs report the authors:

...argue strongly against the vision of a low carbon

> future which is "business as usual but electrified". We want to create a fairer society; one that understands what is involved in producing the resources we consume—not just in terms of fossil fuels but also in terms of land and water use, mineral extraction, labour conditions and the rights of indigenous peoples... The broader societal and economic shifts needed should be understood in the context of the huge and continuing social and economic inequality.[81]

Jeffery calls for the creation of millions of well-paid, trade union jobs to tackle the climate crisis, but emphasises that this also means workers in the old, unsustainable, fossil fuel economy must be "just-transitioned" to new roles. This means that the training and education of a new climate workforce are an integral part of the plans for a just transition. She also points out that only the public sector can deliver the transformative change needed, and the report calls for the "public ownership of the energy sector and the grid, of transport, of the plan to retrofit our homes and buildings and within industry, public ownership of the steel industry and other key sectors".[82]

Without public ownership, private businesses would subordinate a GND or climate jobs programmes to the need to maximise profits. Crucially the Climate Jobs campaign sees workers' struggle as key to winning its demands. As I wrote in the latest edition of the Climate Jobs pamphlet, the participation of workers organisations and trade unions in the 2019 climate strikes "helped build confidence around environmental issues" within the working class movement and makes it "easier to raise demands about climate jobs inside the movement".[83] The question of climate jobs and the transition to the sort of economy envisaged by the report is not an abstract one for trade union and environmental activists:

> The fight for a sustainable future is the struggle of our time. Working people must, through the demand

> for climate jobs that transform the economy, place themselves at the heart of this movement. In doing so we can create an economy that is run in the interests of people and planet.[84]

Plans for alternative, sustainable economies like the Climate Jobs report or the GNDs pose a very specific question for activists - how can they be enacted? Just because a manifesto or plan has the right demands does not mean it will be automatically adopted. In fact the more radical and far-reaching a GND proposal, the more likely it is that the forces of fossil capitalism will oppose it. Right-wing politicians and the fossil fuel industry have blocked even limited attempts to introduce more stringent environmental policies. We also know that the oil industry has been central to undermining climate science and movements through organised denial of climate change. In the face of capitalist intransigence, how can we win radical action on climate change such as Climate Jobs or a socialist Green New Deal? Saltmarsh says that given the short timescale imposed upon us by the climate crisis, there are two strategies the left can pursue:

> We can win state power through democratic elections or seize it through a revolution. We're not in a position for half measures here. Whichever of these two strategies we choose, we should really go all in on it. A revolutionary strategy can be appealing if you have little or no faith in the institutions of capitalist democracy. [85]

Saltmarsh immediately rejects revolution. It would require, he says, violence, winning over the military and police and being ready to occupy "key infrastructure like airports, broadcasting and energy production". [86] He says capitalist societies are "among the most heavily militarised surveillance states history has ever seen" and concludes, "the only strategic option is to build a mass democratic movement for climate justice to win state power at the ballot box" and that the only vehicle for doing this in Britain is the Labour Party.[87] Saltmarsh is guilty of caricaturing what a revolution might look like. He implies that the seizure of power would involve small groups of revolutionaries taking over institutions, buildings and companies in society. Instead revolutionary socialists argue that the workers themselves would seize and control those bodies in a revolution. Workers' power will not come from small groups of dedicated revolutionaries seizing vital capitalist institutions and running them in the name of the working class. It will arise out of a mass movement by workers to take control of their workplaces and social institutions in order to run society in their interests. Rejecting revolution in favour of reforms is not an easier path to socialism. In fact, as we shall see, the reformist path is not a road to socialism at all, but a dead end. It was a point well made by Rosa Luxemburg in 1900:

> People who pronounce themselves in favour of the method of legislative reform in place and in contradistinction to the conquest of political power and social revolution, do not really choose a more tranquil, calmer and slower road to the same goal, but a different goal. Instead of taking a stand for the establishment of a new society they take a stand for surface modifications of the old society.[88]

Given the scale of the climate crisis, understanding how we can win fundamental change is an urgent task. In the next two chapters, we will look more closely at why the capitalist system is so resistant to change and how it protects the interests of the ruling class. This will show us why a reformist strategy that tries to use parliament to bring about a sustainable world is doomed to failure because it cannot challenge the central dynamism of the system. We will begin by looking at how and why capitalism developed into a fossil fuel system before discussing the nature of the capitalist state.

Chapter 4
Fossil fuel capitalism

In this chapter, we will look at how oil, coal and gas became central to capitalism, and how the fossil fuel industry became so powerful. This will help us understand what sort of movement we need to defeat the industry that has been one of the biggest barriers to action on climate change, and, as we saw at COP26, their influence still shapes the global response to the environmental crisis.

Competitive accumulation is what defines capitalism, not the use of fossil fuels. Early capitalist production did not require fossil fuels, and their adoption was the result of class struggle—the interests of the capitalist class conflicting with the interests of the workers. It was because factory and mill owners wanted to improve their exploitation of the workers that they began the transition to fossil fuels. Once a section of the capitalist class did make the transition to production based on fossil fuels, then the whole system shifted in that direction. Competition between the capitalists meant that those who did not adopt fossil fuels faced bankruptcy. As capitalism spread across the globe, it did so as a fossil fuel system. In doing so, vast amounts of wealth has been invested in fossil fuel infrastructure, locking the capitalists further into fossil fuel production. The same logic that forced individual capitalists to adopt fossil fuels now traps them into the system. Capitalism cannot break from fossil fuels—which means the transition away from fossil fuels means a challenge to the very logic of capitalist production.

Sometimes we can believe that industrial economies can only exist with fossil fuels at their heart. Understanding that fossil fuel capitalism is the outcome of a class struggle makes it clear that we could have a society without fossil fuels. Indeed, the struggles of oil, coal and gas workers against the system, shows that those who work in the fossil fuel economy are key allies in the fight for a sustainable society. Understanding how the fossil fuel economy developed gives us one final insight into capitalism—we begin to see the strategic importance of the whole working class.

The centrality of fossil fuels to capitalism becomes obvious when you look at a few statistics. In 2019, 80 percent of US energy came from fossil fuel sources. According to the Statistica website[89] in 2021 the list of the top 15 largest European companies by revenue contains four energy companies (BP, Royal Dutch Shell, Total Energies, Gazprom) and three car companies (VW, Daimler, BMW). An eighth company, Glencore, is a trading and mining company that has significant interests in coal. Glencore expects to increase coal production by 14 percent in 2022, and make a predicted $6 billion in revenue.[90] The total wealth of some of these companies is staggering. BP, for instance, had a net income in 2021 of $8.5 billion and total assets of over $287 billion.[91] Fossil fuels, and associated industries, are big business.

The value of these fossil fuel companies indicates their centrality to modern capitalism, but it was not automatic that capitalism adopted coal, oil and gas. Indeed, before the 19th century fossil fuels were peripheral to capitalist production. Early capitalist manufacturing relied on human and animal work or water and wind power. Nonetheless, because of the decisions made by mill and factory owners in 19th century England, manufacturing became dependent on coal and eventually oil and gas and shaped the further development of capitalism. In particular, they set in motion the climate crisis we are experiencing today.

To understand how these fuels become locked into the

capitalist economy, we need to remind ourselves that the capitalist's sole source of surplus value is the labour of human beings. In order to maximise their profits, capitalists have a number of ways of extracting more surplus value from workers. One way that they could do this was through the introduction of machinery. As capitalism developed, manufacturing went through a process of change. Originally, production took place in small, family based units. Eventually production switched to larger manufactories, such as mills, powered by water wheels. Then the capitalists introduced steam engines to power more and more machines, in larger and larger factories.

In Britain, the capitalists became adept at applying technology to their production methods.[92] The Industrial Revolution saw rapid scientific breakthroughs and technological innovation as capitalism constantly revolutionised production. These changes did not benefit everyone. Industrial development shattered old ways of working and living. New industries arose, and then disappeared, destroying whole communities as the capitalists constantly adapted production in the interest of profit. The growing importance of industrial machines also saw the workforce subordinated to the technology.

Marx pointed out how machinery transformed production and social relations:

> Modern industry never views or treats the existing form of a production process as the definitive one... By means of machinery, chemical process and other methods, [capitalism] is continually transforming not only the technical basis of production but also the functions of the worker and the social combinations of the labour process. At the same time, it thereby also revolutionises the division of labour within society, and incessantly throws masses of capital and of workers from one branch of production to another.[93]

The evolution of "large-scale industry" removes all

"security" from the workers who are constantly having to adapt to the whims of the capitalist, and are frequently thrown into unemployment.[94] Key to this process however were the workers, and it was the need for workers that made the steam engine (and its fuel) attractive to the capitalists.

Today the invention of the steam engine is synonymous with the Industrial Revolution. Initially they were used for pumping water out of mines rather than driving factory machinery. The Industrial Revolution did not require the steam engine to start it, in fact the Industrial Revolution made the steam engine possible. As Marx explains:

> The steam-engine itself, such as it was at its invention during the manufacturing period at the close of the seventeenth century, and such as it continued to be down to 1780, did not give rise to any industrial revolution. It was, on the contrary, the invention of machines that made a revolution in the form of steam-engines necessary.[95]

The Industrial Revolution would have happened without steam power—the capitalists had sources of energy such as water and wind which allowed them to power large factories. It was the need of the capitalist class to better exploit workers' labour that saw them adopt steam power. Of course, steam power offered huge benefits over other sources of energy. In *Capital* Marx showed how developing industry saw the capitalists move away from human and animal power to more reliable sources. Wind, another early and common source of power for windmills was, he noted, "too inconstant and uncontrollable" for large-scale industry so "in England, the birthplace of large-scale industry, the use of water-power preponderated even during the period of manufacture".[96]

But water power too had its limitations. As Marx explains the "flow of water could not be increased at will, it failed at certain seasons of the year, and above all it was essentially local".[97] The steam engine allowed the factory owner to break free from all of these constraints.

> Not till the invention of Watt's second... steam-engine was a prime mover [a source of mechanical motion] found which drew its own motive power from the consumption of coal and water, was entirely under man's control, was mobile and a means of locomotion, was urban and not—like the water-wheel—rural, permitted production to be concentrated in towns instead of—like the water-wheels—being scattered over the countryside and, finally, was of universal technical application, and little affected in its choice of residence by local circumstances.[98]

What Marx identifies here is that the switch to steam power had huge benefits over waterpower. However, the most important consequence was that the capitalists were no longer constrained to the countryside where most rivers were, and could move production into the cities where the workers were. The question of workers was always a major preoccupation for the capitalists. Because coal could be transported to anywhere it was needed, steam power allowed the capitalist to build factories and mills where the workers' were located. [99] In his brilliant history of the development of fossil fuel capitalism, Andreas Malm argues steam was a "ticket to the town" for the capitalists. He quotes J R McCulloch, one of Scotland's foremost economists, writing in 1833:

> The real advantage of the application of the power of steam to give motion to the machinery of a spinning mill, or of a number of power-looms, appears to be a good deal misapprehended. It does not consist so much in any direct saving of labour, as in permitting it to be carried on in the most proper situation. The work that is done by the aid of a stream of water, is

> generally as cheap as that which is done by steam, and sometimes cheaper. But the invention of the steam-engine has relieved us from the necessity of building factories in inconvenient situations merely for the sake of a waterfall. It has allowed them to be placed in the centre of a population trained to industrious habits.[100]

The capitalists made the decision to move their factories to the urban areas, even when the cost of power from steam was much higher than obtaining the same driving force from water. Again, Malm quotes the Scottish hydraulic engineer Robert Thom in 1834 noting that costs of steam power in Glasgow were seven times those of waterpower in rural Greenock for one manufacturer, but the move to Glasgow gave the owners "a trained population ready for such factories".[101]

It also relieved factory owners of the burden of having to provide homes and provisions for their workers. Because of its "spatial fixity", waterpower, as Malm perceptively notes, required a factory owner to "form personal relations to his hands".[102] In the town the owner no longer had to pay the cost of housing and looking after their employees, and workers could be easily replaced by the mass of unemployed outside the factory gates—a bonus which undermined the organising ability of the workers. The ability to better exploit labour is a key reason why the switch to fossil fuel production took place so quickly—in a matter of a couple of decades.

The transition to a fossil fuel economy was not automatic. At each stage, ordinary people contested changes that meant they would lose their livelihoods or see the destruction of their communities. The early development of capitalism required the destruction of old forms of social organisation. In the English countryside this saw the systematic "expropriation and expulsion of the agricultural population" through a brutal process of enclosure and the destruction of traditional rural social organisation. The enclosure of farmland and the destruction of the commons was in part about the rationalisation, in the interest of capital, of the rural landscape as well as the creation of wage labour—in the fields, or the newly industrialising towns.[103]

These developments took place in parallel with a global transformation. Marx wrote that the "discovery of gold and silver in America, the extirpation, enslavement and entombment in mines of the indigenous population of that continent, the beginnings of the conquest and plunder of India, and the conversion of Africa into a preserve for the commercial hunting of blackskins, are all things which characterize the dawn of the era of capitalist production".[104]

In order for capitalism to transform the world, it had to overcome resistance from below. Ordinary people in rural England fought enclosure and the loss of their common lands. Artisans who worked in household industries based on family production resisted the transition to industrial manufacturing. As capitalism developed, workers fought to protect their interests, wages, historic rights and traditional working practices. Indigenous people fought to resist the spread of capitalism through colonialism to their regions.

Josiah Wedgwood had to defeat the "customary norms that had prohibited certain market behaviours" in order for his pottery manufacturing to become the phenomenal success that it was.[105] Elsewhere in England, the industrial capitalist class had to defeat workers such as the Luddites (1811) and the Captain Swing movement (1830) two risings against the introduction of job-destroying machines.[106] These risings were not against technology as such, but the use of machines to maximise profit through reductions in numbers of workers. They are part of a much longer tradition. An early example of these struggles saw the destruction in 1791 of a 400-loom steam powered factory in Manchester just a few weeks after their installation.[107]

The new machines, and their fuel, also became the site for class struggle. As early as the 1640s coal miners in south west England fought to protect their mining rights.[108] As coal became increasingly central to capitalist production, those who mined and transported it came to have significant power. In 1842 the

Miners' Association of Great Britain and Ireland was formed from an intense period of class struggle that saw workers directly tackling steam power.[109]

The year has been described as the "the grimmest year of the nineteenth century" a period of high unemployment, economic depression, high prices and low wages.[110] It saw the first general strike in history, involving up to half a million workers. One of the key features of this strike was the workers' targeting of steam engines. The pulling of the plugs from boilers gave rise to the movement's popular name: the Plug Plot riots. Workers understood that the engines powered the factories and mills, and in sabotaging them, they were shutting down production. Workers' were using the control of fossil fuels to demonstrate their power.[111] Malm quotes from an account of the strike spreading to Stockport, reported in the *Bradford Observer* on 18 August 1842:

> In several instances, where any hesitation was evinced in stopping the mills, portions of the mob entered the premises, and pulled the fires from under the boilers, which shortly caused the moving power to a stand still. Every steam-engine in the borough was shortly stopped: and the hatters, moulders, calico-printers, tailors, and every other trade were soon idle. [112]

Hundreds, perhaps thousands, of such incidents took place in 1842. Malm quotes examples of strikers targeting boilers and chanting "stop the smoke" as they protested across the north west and says "It should be clear that 'plug drawing'—shorthand for a repertoire of acts of sabotage against steam engines—was not incidental, but constitutive of the general strike".[113]

The number of these events gives us an indication of the scale of the new fossil fuel economy, and the importance of steam power to it. The story of the 1842 strike also shows that workers understood that fossil fuel infrastructure was simultaneously part of their exploitation but also a weakness of capitalism that they could exploit. As Malm concludes, "the working class could impose its will on capital by closing the spigots of the fossil fuel economy".[114]

This was a lesson learnt by workers and capitalists alike. Turning off the fossil fuel spigot would become a key weapon of workers whether directly employed in the fossil fuel industry or not. The struggle between workers and capital over the next 100 years saw thousands of other examples were fossil fuel infrastructure became a site for struggle.

By the 20th century, the importance of coal and oil to capitalism meant that some of the greatest workers' struggles were centred on the control of fossil fuel. For example, in 1972, British miners in the National Union of Mineworkers (NUM) launched a major strike over pay. Because the strike stopped the production of coal, it threatened capitalist production immediately. For both sides, winning or losing the strike centred on whether or not coal would continue to reach the power stations, which drove the economy. Other unions showed solidarity by preventing the movement and burning of coal. As Pete Jackson explains:

> From the beginning the National Union of Railwaymen blacked [the refusal to touch or move goods affected by a strike] the pits and power stations, dramatically reducing the movements of coal... ASLEF, the train drivers' union, told their members not to move anything unusual. The docks were solid, refusing to move imported coal. The Transport and General Workers Union lorry drivers were solid, refusing to cross picket lines... in many areas coal, oil and anything useful in a power station stopped moving.[115]

The strike was marked by militant rank and file action, solidarity from the wider working class and, in particular, mass picketing. A particular focus of the strike was a coking plant in Saltley, Birmingham. The plant was one of the few places still producing and distributing fuel and the miners were determined to shut it down. Arthur Scargill, then a union official in Yorkshire, but later the leader of the NUM, described how the miners saw Saltley:

> I have never even seen anything like it in my life. It was like the most gigantic stack of any colliery that I'd ever seen. It was estimated that there were a million tons; it was like a mountain. This was no coke depot in the accepted sense. It was an Eldorado of coke. There were a thousand lorries a day going in.

Shutting down the Saltley plant became a key battle for the miners. Despite thousands of miners trying to shut the plant down, they were unable to do this in the face of brutal police violence. Scargill and other activists spoke at meetings around the West Midlands. Scargill demanded "physical support; we wanted strike action". [116] On Thursday 10 February, workers across Birmingham walked out on strike and descended in their thousands on Saltley. Despite 700 police, mass picketing shut the plant down.

Jackson notes that the significance of the "Battle of Saltley Gate" is not just that the action stopped the distribution of coke. Mass solidarity by 30,000 striking workers shifted the balance of forces. It was a "lesson of militancy and solidarity [that] would be learned across the working class". [117] Thousands of workers actively took part in shutting down the lifeblood of capitalist production.

Two years later, the then Tory Prime Minister Edward Heath called a general election in the midst of strikes and a three-day week. Heath framed the election as being about "who governs?" The election resulted in a hung parliament and a further election later in the year saw Heath's defeat. The miners' showed that workers' militancy could determine "who governed".

The workers' understood the centrality of the fossil fuels to production and so did the capitalists. In 1972 the British government had told the police to keep the Saltley plant open at all costs, though they failed in this task. In 1979 Margaret Thatcher's government came to power and set about planning to take on the most powerful sections of the British working class.

In 1984, Margaret Thatcher's government provoked a fight with the NUM, but this time they prepared the ground. Stockpiling coal and coke, they also awarded pay rises to unions that had previously shown solidarity with the NUM, hoping to make them less likely to strike. After a year-long strike, the NUM was defeated; a loss that still reverberates through the British trade union movement today.

Despite the importance of coal to the British economy, Thatcher's Tory government was prepared to close pits and destroy the industry (alongside the wrecking of the lives of thousands of working people) because it was more important to break the strength of one of the most powerful sections of the union movement. Instead of coal Thatcher's government encouraged a transition to other forms of energy generation—North Sea oil and gas, and nuclear power.[118]

The power of workers in the fossil fuel industry—miners, workers in the oil industry and power stations and those that transport these fuels—has been demonstrated time and again. South African coal miners were central to the fight against apartheid. During the Iranian Revolution oil workers were a core part of the mass strikes that forced the US friendly ruler, the Shah, to grant major concessions: 70,000 of them took part in the February 1979 strikes that led to the collapse of the monarchy.[119]

Just as in 1842 and 1972, these workers understood the importance of fossil fuels to the capitalist economy, and used their power to turn off the supply or hamper its distribution. To be clear the argument here is not that *only* fossil fuel workers have power to challenge capitalism. However, the nature of fossil fuel capitalism creates a weakness that all sections of the workers' movement can use. We will return to the power of workers *as a class* later in this book.

Once one group of capitalists adopted fossil fuels it gave them significant advantages over other capitalists, and because of the competition between capitals, it meant that other capitalists soon followed suit. This process took place remarkably quickly. Malm identifies a rapid transition to a fossil fuel economy in Britain between 1830 and 1854. These years saw the "highest rate of growth in coal production ever experienced" as well as the fastest growth of steam power. In 1830 the largest demand for coal was for heating homes, by 1855 the transition to a coal centred economy meant 57 percent of domestic demand for coal was for manufacturing plus iron and steel production, compared to 25 percent for home heating. By 1860 most water mills had disappeared.[120]

The global spread of the fossil fuel economy

Fossil fuels became essential as a source of power in every industry, but they also became crucial for the rest of the economy. Everything from agriculture to power generation came to rely on the burning of coal, oil or gas. This new fossil fuel reality was the "unique creation" of British capitalists.[121] It rapidly spread around the world. As Ian Angus has explained:

> In 1825 [Britain] was producing 80 percent of the world's greenhouse gas emissions from fossil fuel combustion, and in 1850 it was still generating 62 percent—twice as much as the United States, France, Germany and Belgium combined. Between 1850 and 1873, Britain's coal consumption tripled, from 37 million to 112 million tons; France's jumped from 7 million to nearly 25 million tons; and Germany's rose from 5 million to 36 million.[122]

Fossil fuels quickly became essential for colonial powers so they could impose their will on their colonies. In time, imperialist nations needed fossil fuels to subjugate the rest of the world, and sourcing and protecting access to fossil fuels became an imperialist object. Mass transport, powered by coal and, eventually oil, helped the capitalist class to put down revolt and extend their interests. Coal in particular helped colonial powers reshape the world in their interests.

The Industrial Revolution saw a new age of military force powered by coal. For the first time railways became an important commercial and military asset. Christian Wolmar notes that in 1830 the newly opened Manchester to Liverpool line, the first railway line in the world, was used to send a regiment to the docks in Liverpool for transport to Ireland to quell a rebellion. The trip reduced the journey time from two days to two hours.

In 1846 the world's first "significant" use of railways for the military saw the transport of "14,500 Prussian soldiers, together with their horses and wagons, to smash the Krakow rebellion of Polish nationalists". Two years later the Russian Tsar used the Warsaw to Vienna line to send troops to help crush a rebellion in Hungary.[123] Railways were crucial to the victory of the Union over the Confederacy in the US Civil War. As Angus notes it was military possibilities that led governments to "subsidize coal mining and railway building with cash, land grants, and large military contracts".[124]

On the seas and oceans steam power saw gunboats deployed to protect and extend colonial interests. Fossil fuels meant that colonial power could get to places hitherto out of reach, or enable navies to break free of the limits imposed by weather.

In their book *White Skin, Black Fuel*, Andreas Malm and the Zetkin Collective recount the first use of the steam gunboat by a British Navy squadron sent to defeat a rebellious Egyptian ruler Muhammad Ali. Ali wanted an Egyptian cotton industry, which threatened British profits. The British used their new steamboats to destroy Ali's forces. A year later steam proved crucial to British victory in the First Opium War. Malm and the Zetkin Collective quote from the *Observer* newspaper, "Steam, even now, almost realises the idea of military omnipotence and military omnipresence; it is everywhere, and there is no withstanding it".[125]

Malm and the Zetkin Collective note that the adoption of fossil fuels increased the military power of the British Empire, and helped to fuel a racist narrative of superiority over the people of the Global South. In 1830 for instance, two explorers mapping the Niger River claimed that the steam engine was a "fit means of conveying civilisation among these uninformed Africans".[126] Such was the centrality of fossil fuels to founding and protecting the British Empire that Malm and his co-authors argue, "modern racism... is unthinkable without techno-racism". They explain that:

> No technological complex was as pivotal as this one: the steamboats, the railroad cars and all the other steam-powered machines of white Europe. Travellers boarded them on triumphal processions through the colonies and sent home word of the shock and awe.

Steamboat navies furthered an "ecological imperialism" that saw colonial powers steal natural resources, people and wealth from around the world.[127] The use of fossil-fuelled military power also enabled the securing of further fossil fuels. Malm and the Zetkin Collective say that when Europeans arrived on Vancouver Island, one of the first things they did was to "uncover seams of coal".[128]

Military needs, and the fear of workers' revolt, eventually drove a naval energy transition. The decision of the British Navy to convert its fleets from coal to oil occurred because the admiralty feared that miners' strikes might hamper the navy's ability to fight.[129] The two world wars saw oil become a key strategic resource for the global economy. The planes, ships, submarines, tanks and lorries that were produced in vast quantities needed oil which helped make sure that the oil fields of the Caucasus and the Middle East were strategic targets. In the aftermath of the Second World War, the United States used the Marshall Plan to impose its own interests on Europe. This tied economic support for European recovery to US oil. The

US forced European countries to purchase expensive oil from the US, which "accelerated Europe's long-term transition from dependence on coal to dependence on oil".[130]

The first half of the 20thcentury also saw the transformation of European agriculture. By the end of the Second World War, British agriculture had become highly dependent on oil—particularly to power tractors, but also for the production of chemical inputs like fertiliser and pesticides. The post-war period saw French agriculture completely mechanised, with a corresponding transformation in farm and field size.[131] Similar changes in Britain saw social relations in farming transformed as tractors and other machinery reduced workforces.[132]

The industrialisation of agriculture also saw the massive increase in the use of artificial pesticides and fertilisers. These chemicals relied on fossil fuels for their manufacturer—both for energy and because they were often based on oil. Oil companies like Shell expanded into the manufacture of agricultural chemicals.

In their history of the British oil industry, James Marriott and Terry Macalister explain that for Shell pesticides were a perfect product. They were "well protected by patents, hydro-carbon-based, and research-intensive; they were modern and glamorous in offering an instant, technical solution to ancient scourges of mankind, they fitted in well with other manufacturing processes; and they combined low volume with stupendously hard margins". These chemicals were supposed to free farmers from the threat of pests and disease, but quickly became associated with ecological damage and dangers to humans and farming.[133] The family of pesticides known as "drins" had their origins in arms manufacturing during the Second World War. In 1950 the oil company Shell obtained sole rights to their manufacture. Drins and other hydrocarbon-based pesticides such as DDT where among the chemicals discussed in Rachel Carson's pioneering ecological work *Silent Spring*. She showed how even tiny amounts of these highly toxic chemicals were concentrated through ecosystems with disastrous impacts for plants, animals and humans.[134] Carson's exposé of the dangers of these chemicals and the ensuring public campaign saw them being banned in Britain and the USA. But the oil companies were unwilling to forego all their profits, and as Marriott and Macalister point out, a "two-tier colonial operation" took place as Shell continued to manufacture these deadly chemicals in the Global South, until their eventual global ban in 2001.[135]

The global fossil fuel economy arose out of the needs of capitalism. Once capitalism in Britain had become addicted to fossil fuels, capitalism everywhere developed along the same lines. At the same time, Britain and other industrial nations were able to use fossil fuels militarily to strengthen their grip on their colonies and expand their own interests.

Fossil fuels became central to an imperialist system that imposed capitalism on the globe. Those military forces were then deployed to ensure that the Global North, in particular the United States, maintained control over oil resources. The history of imperialism in the 20th and 21st century has been the story of how the Global North used fossil fuels to subjugate the rest of the world. The logic of capitalist accumulation saw the system adopt fossil fuels and burn them in vast quantities to maximise profits. The fossil fuel industry made sure that every aspect of the economy, from the military to agriculture, from transport to packaging became dependent on oil, coal and gas. What happened when the world began to be aware that doing this drove ecological disaster?

Climate denial

It is striking that the fossil fuel industry was aware of the danger of global warming long before almost everyone else, understanding that climate change was real, and a threat to their profits. They needed a strategy to protect themselves, so they started by denying the problem. Scientist Michael E. Mann has described the ensuing propaganda assault as a "Climate War". It saw the creation of a machine of climate denial, so strong that the most technologically and scientifically advanced country in the world, the United States, saw Donald Trump, a climate denier sitting in the Whitehouse.

It is worth exploring a little about precisely what the oil companies knew about climate change because it makes clear that they consciously put profits before people and planet. In 1959 physicist Edward Teller spoke at a symposium marking the centenary of the American oil industry. Teller explained that the continued burning of fossil fuels would add to the carbon dioxide in the atmosphere. Carbon dioxide has, he said, a "strange property… its presence in the atmosphere causes a greenhouse effect". He warned that by the end of the 20th century the warming would melt the ice caps and "submerge New York". Teller emphasised "all the coastal cities would be covered, and since a considerable percentage of the human race lives in coastal regions, I think this contamination is more serious than most people tend to believe".[136] These were not passing remarks, indeed in the published account of his speech, Teller responds to questions by emphasising the threat from the melting ice caps.[137]

Teller's 1959 speech was not the only opportunity the oil industry had to learn about the greenhouse effect in the 1950s. Studies in the 1950s run by the American Petroleum Institute (API) and Exxon's predecessor company Humble Oil were showing that fossil fuels were leading to increased carbon dioxide in the atmosphere. Further studies in the 1960s, 1970s and 1980s were making it very clear that oil companies were causing a major problem. By 1980 oil companies including Exxon, Texaco and Shell concluded that the planet faced "globally catastrophic effects" by 2067.[138]Through the 1980s and 1990s and then into the 2000s fossil fuel corporations were responsible for funding organisations that systematically undermined climate science and scientists. The formation of the IPCC took place in 1988, the same year that companies like ExxonMobil, Shell, BP, Chevron and the API created the Heartland Institute.[139] Organisations like these existed solely to systematically create uncertainty about climate change.

Every time you hear a journalist or politician talk about climate change as a "scientific debate", they are echoing the words of these think tanks. As Michael E Mann has said, the "forces of inaction—that is the fossil fuel interests and those doing their bidding—have a single goal—inaction".[140] Today climate denial has evolved into different forms, indeed most fossil fuel companies no longer deny the science, and instead focus on greenwashing their businesses or claim to be developing new technologies to prevent emissions. Some of the most fervent climate deniers now are politicians from the far-right and fascist movements—something explored in detail recently by Malm and the Zetkin Collective. These researchers show there are close links between right-wing climate denial and racism, and a historic obsession of the right with fossil fuel energy.[141]

The victory of right-wing politicians often sees the rolling back of legislation designed to transition away from fossil fuels. Fossil fuel companies are quick to leap back and restore their profits. It is not enough to elect environmentally aware, left-wing politicians. Change must be permanent, which requires breaking up the fossil fuel economy itself.

But the interests of the capitalist state and its associated capitals—the companies and multinational corporations in a particular country—are closely aligned. Both the capitalists and their state will organise to prevent challenges to their interests. This will mean stopping action that hampers accumulation, but also preventing change that might affect the core part of the capitalist economy. In order to understand how we can win fundamental change we will now need to look at how the state works and the sort of movements needed to challenge, and defeat it.

Chapter 5
The capitalist state

Capitalism is an economic system based on the exploitation of the mass of the population by a tiny minority. As a minority, the capitalist class needs to organise to protect itself, and its interests, from the majority of the population whose interests lie in overthrowing them. This chapter is about how they do it.

The capitalist state—the collective name for the institutions, from the police and military, to the law courts and prisons—appears to stand neutrally above society, but in fact enforces the status quo.

Friedrich Engels explained the role of the state:

> It is a product of society at a particular stage of development; it is the admission that this society has involved itself in insoluble self-contradiction and is cleft into irreconcilable antagonisms which it is powerless to exorcise. But in order that these antagonisms, classes with conflicting economic interests, shall not consume themselves and society in fruitless struggle, a power, apparently standing above society, has become necessary to moderate the conflict and keep it within the bounds of "order"; and this power, arisen out of society, but placing itself above it and increasingly alienating itself from it, is the state.[142]

The state consists of institutions and laws, but, above all, it rests on what Russian revolutionary Lenin called "special bodies of armed men". The state can deploy these forces—police, soldiers, prisons, laws, magistrates, judges and courts—against those who want to challenge the system. The capitalist class has these forces in reserve so it can use violence, or the threat of violence, to maintain its rule.

The state institutions do not sit neutrally above society arbitrating between the interests of workers and capitalists. They actively engage in protecting and extending the interests of the ruling class.

As the US Marxist Hal Draper explained:

> The state is the institution, or complex of institutions, which bases itself on the availability of forcible coercion by special agencies of society in order to maintain the dominance of a ruling class, preserve existing property relations from basic change, and keep all other classes in subjection.[143]

The state relies on the "availability" of force, but it does not always use it. Keeping "classes in subjection", more generally means "in willing compliance, in passive acquiescence, or in ingrained dependence", but occasionally force is needed. Governments can use state institutions to ban protests, arrest strikers, beat and imprison revolutionaries or kill their enemies.

The development of the state

The state is not unique to capitalism—states have arisen whenever a ruling class has needed to protect its interests from wider society. States developed at a particularly point in human history—with the rise of class society. Which means that for the majority of human existence there were no states, as there were no contending classes.

For most of human history, people lived as hunter-gatherers in small non-hierarchical communal groups. We know that social relations were characterised by cooperation, the sharing of tasks and a far less rigid set of gender roles. In such societies, there was no need for state coercion or a resort to violence to maintain the status quo. Once differing interests between different groups began to manifest in society this changed. [144] The key change that allowed this to happen was the development of agriculture, which allowed the production of a surplus of food.[145]

With a surplus of food, it was possible—though not inevitable—that a minority of people could take control of the extra food and use it in their interests. We know that many historical societies developed cultural ways of preventing the development of hierarchies or minority rule. Indeed sometimes the leaders or "big men" who rose to prominence, used their control of the surplus to help the whole community, rather than for personal gain.

As Kent Flannery and Joyce Marcus explain:

> Most horticultural tribes still valued the generosity and reciprocal gift-giving we saw in hunting-and-gathering societies. Indeed, these behaviours escalated in societies with lineages, clans, and moieties [a group of clans], because now each of these larger units had reciprocal relations with others".[146]

A surplus of food from agriculture was the prerequisite for the development of class society. But classes did not arise automatically or inevitably—they developed out of concrete historical circumstances. Chris Harman links the rise of class society to the development of what Marx called the "productive forces". As social relations changed in a society, some in that society began to identify their interests as benefiting from the exploitation of the labour of others and the private control of natural resources. This group...

> ...defends that control even when that means making others suffer. It comes to see social advance as

> embodied in itself and in the protection of its own livelihood against sudden outbreaks of scarcity... that cause enormous hardship to everybody else.[147]

For a group in society to own and control the surplus food required them using some of the surplus to employ people in non-producing roles—such as priests or guards. Others might be employed to collect taxes or to help this new class rule in other ways. The development of class society did not happen because humans are naturally greedy, it was a consequence of specific historical conditions—and many societies actively organised to prevent such hierarchies developing. Nonetheless, once a minority did control the surplus, they could convert it to private property and use it for personal gain.

So the need for a class to control surplus food and wealth can led to the development of "armed bodies of man" to guard the surplus from the rest of society and in turn protect the emerging ruling class. Others people might be employed to monitor food supplies, tax the rest of the population or settle disputes. From such beginnings, we see the emergence of the state alongside a ruling class and an exploited class.

The ruling class pays the individuals who are part of the state well in order to keep them loyal. These functionaries are then more willing to push the interests of the ruling class, and through their higher pay feel an affinity to the ruling class when compared to the working class. Part of the reason the ruling class pays its functionaries well is to create a separation between them and the wider population.

Under capitalism soldiers live in their barracks away from the wider population, police officers are routinely paid higher wages than workers and usually live far from the communities they patrol.

Physically isolating state forces from the wider working class and paying them more than workers means that they are less likely to identify with the interests of workers and their communities. Such separation makes it easier for the authorities to deploy force against striking or rebellious workers—something we have seen on many occasions during workers' rebellions. For instance, when the Chinese government used soldiers to destroy the democracy movement in Tiananmen Square in 1989, they were careful to use regiments based far from the capital city.

How the state behaves

For the state to have authority in society, it must give the appearance of acting in the interests of everyone. In both ancient class societies and modern capitalism, the state provides social functions that superficially appear to benefit all. A modern state might provide healthcare, education and sanitation for instance. These are social functions that "may take on the appearance of non-class functions even in a class-bound state".[148] However, they cannot be separated from wider class interests. Education under capitalism for working class pupils prepares them for the world of wage labour. Healthcare is geared towards producing a fit and healthy working class, and historically sanitation was usually introduced only when the spread of disease undermined profits.

The state also has to fulfil an ideological role in the sense it has to convey a message that it applies to everyone equally. While big corporations have accountants who help them evade tax, legally at least, everyone in society has to abide by the rules. The law is supposed to apply equally to everyone, even though the rich can often buy the best legal representation to get them out of trouble, while working people cannot afford a decent defence. The state must appear to be neutral, because if it did not then the mask would slip and the majority of people would get an insight into its real function.

It is worth considering one other aspect to the state's behaviour in this context. Marx and Engels wrote: "The executive of the modern state is but a committee for managing the common affairs of the whole bourgeoisie".[149] What they meant was that the state, while organising in the collective interest of the ruling class, also had to manage the competition between capitalists.

Without some level of organisation, capitalist production would descend into chaos, so the state must also "mediate, reconcile, in some way settle the internecine disputes and conflicts within the ruling class".[150] This might mean creating laws to govern how the market works, or supporting particular industries.

It also means that a state will intervene on the international level in the interests of its country's capitalists. Sometimes this might mean going to war—over access to raw materials, markets or in defence of wider interests. It also means negotiating with other nation-states over the division of global resources. Here we return to the question of the environment. Differing national interests shape the arguments inside COP climate conferences. In 2009 at COP15 in Copenhagen, US President Obama led a grouping of wealthy countries to impose the "Copenhagen Accords" which directly benefited US capital by undermining a more radical agreement. The way that powerful economies, dominated by fossil fuel capital, can shape the outcome of climate conferences is one reason the UN's process is so flawed—and it has its origins in the way states defend the interests of capital.

Why we cannot reform the state

The state is more than just organised "bodies of armed men". These however do remain in reserve while capitalism favours more subtle forms of coercion and control. Capitalism has a whole range of weapons in its armoury to undermine challenges from below. The system uses sexism, racism, homophobia and transphobia to divide workers against each other. Our education system tells us that capitalism is the natural way of organising society. We are encouraged to believe that humans are greedy by nature and competition rather than cooperation is normal.

The law itself, while appearing to apply equally to everyone, arises out of the interests of the capitalists. Capitalism's obsession with private property, the accumulation of capital and so on, is associated with a system of laws that reflect these priorities. The very birth of capitalism saw the destruction of old social, economic and legal arrangements in the interest of the new society. The creation of new institutions furthered these interests. Rafts of new laws transformed how people could use land, natural resources and their labour. The new capitalist state introduced new forms of policing to make sure everyone kept their place in the new society. Those that tried to live outside of capitalism, rejected its priorities, broke its laws or rebelled were criminalised and punished.

There are other subtle ways of control. The parliamentary system offers the illusion of participation and democracy for workers. We are told that there is no need to protest, strike or revolt; instead, we can choose politicians who will enact change for us. Superficially, the parliamentary system appears to give us all equality—almost everyone has a vote, and almost everyone can stand for election. However, the system is skewed towards the wealthy—my single vote counts for little against the influence of media baron Rupert Murdoch. Even when radical politicians are elected aiming to reform the system, they find that the capitalist state will act against them.

A particular capitalist state will be closely associated with particular companies. This is very clear with oil companies, where companies like BP and Shell or ExxonMobile or Chevron are closely associated with Britain and the US. This is not just restricted to fossil fuel companies—major corporations and multinationals develop in particular countries and are thus closely associated with the interests of those nation-states. This means that there is a close link between the interests of those capitals and the state itself.

This intertwining of state and capital means they have what Chris Harman has called a "structural interdependence" of shared interests. As Harman explains:

> The particular capitals find it easier to operate within one state rather than another, because they may have to profoundly restructure both their internal organisation and their relations with other capitals if they move their operations. The state has to adjust to the needs of

> particular capitals because it depends on them for the resources—particularly the revenues from taxation—it needs to keep going: if it goes against their interests, they can move their liquid assets abroad.[151]

There is also an overlap between state and capital. Politicians who lose their seats often move to lucrative positions in multinational corporations, or sit on boards while in office. These close links were on display at COP26 when national delegations took representatives of their fossil fuel companies to Glasgow.

The capitalist state is not neutral. It arises out of the needs of the ruling class and the interests of their capitalist system. It is an instrument of class rule used by the capitalist class to further their interests and maintain their position. This is why it cannot be seized and used by the working class. Despite this, many on the left hope that the state can be reformed so that radical change can come through parliament. Their argument is that it can be reorganised in the interest of the majority, and used to improve working class lives with major reforms.

But getting socialists elected to parliament does not change the nature, or the personnel, of the state. Despite the close links between individual politicians and particular corporations, the replacement of one set of politicians by another leaves the structure and personnel in place.

With a change in government, it is remarkably striking how little changes in the state. The unelected civil servants, bosses and generals who determine much of what happens in society remain in place. We cannot vote out Richard Branson, Rupert Murdoch, Elon Musk or Jeff Bezos. The electorate does not choose the Generals, Admirals and Air Marshalls of the army, navy and air force. Indeed politicians do not even select most of these figures. The people who make decisions to close factories, hire and fire workers and cut wages are usually the capitalists, not MPs. In fact there is very little democratic control of the forces in society that make key decisions that affect the lives of millions of people. This is not to say that elections do not matter, but to recognise that parliament has limited control over society as a whole.

A socialist society is one where every institution in society is under workers control. Achieving that will not come through parliamentary reforms. Instead, socialists have to contrast a different state to the existing capitalist one. For Marx and Engels, the very definition of a state is that it is an instrument of class rule, the "product of the irreconcilability of class contradictions" and this would also be true of the workers' state.

Marx and Engels argued for the creation of a workers' state through revolution. The revolution would smash the capitalist state and replace it with a workers' state, which in turn would defend the majority of the population against the capitalist class's attempts to regain control.

Which would be suppressing the old order. With the final defeat of the capitalist class, Marx argued that the state would "wither away". We shall return to these concepts later.

*

In his strategy for winning a socialist Green New Deal, Saltmarsh rightly argues, "perhaps the biggest barrier to climate justice is the resistance of capital".[152] Saltmarsh also acknowledges that only the state can implement the sort of action that can tackle climate change. He says, only the...

> ...state has the power to regulate, penalise or dismantle corporations. It also has the power to nationalise companies or whole sectors of the economy or create new companies able to compete with private ones. That the state is the only political body with the power to confront capital is argument enough on its own for the need to use state power for climate justice.

He concludes, "if we could direct state capacity to work for these ends... we at least give ourselves a chance"[153] and says that "those committed to climate justice should get serious about strategies for capturing state power".[154] However, the question for socialists has to be *what sort* of state can do this?

The forces of capitalism will resist any reforms that pose a challenge to corporate profit or the existence of fossil fuel capital. Nationalisation of oil companies or the dismantling of the coal industry would certainly fall into this category. Saltmarsh says that this requires us to ask, "who's in charge"? But, for socialists "who is in charge" is about much more than who is sitting in Downing Street or the Whitehouse. It is about who has *power* in society.

A left-wing government might take *office* under capitalism, but it will not have *power* unless institutions are created that can be a direct challenge to the capitalist state itself. Capitalism will often allow reforms, particularly if they benefit capital itself—the British National Health Service is a good example of this. Anything more fundamental will be opposed—violently if need be. This is why enacting radical change does not simply pose the question of who is in charge. It poses the question of workers' power against capitalism.

The history of the socialist movement is littered with examples of left-wing governments that attempted to introduce changes, but found themselves constrained by the capitalist system they sought to reform. The most recent example of this is from Greece in the 2010s. In the aftermath of the 2008 economic crash, the left party Syriza was elected promising to end austerity. It immediately found itself trapped by the logic of the market. The "Troika", the European Commission, European Central Bank and the International Monetary Fund, forced Syriza into a corner. Syriza's leaders were faced with a choice—either compromise with capitalism and continue enacting austerity or unleash social forces to challenge the logic of capital. Syriza's leaders were unwilling to take on the system and ended up imposing further austerity on the Greek working class.

In Britain we are well aware, from the smears used against

left-wing Labour leader Jeremy Corbyn, how the media, the state and big business will treat a socialist politician even before they get close to government.

Tragically, history also tells us that attempts to bring about far-reaching change through Parliament also risk bloody retribution against the left and the workers' movement. An instructive example comes from Chile in 1972-3 where a reformist government found itself destroyed by the capitalist state with tens of thousands of workers' paying the price.

Chile

In September 1970, Salvador Allende won Chile's presidential election. Allende was a left reformist politician who led Popular Unity (UP), a coalition of social democratic parties such as the Socialist Party of Chile (of which Allende was a lifelong member), the Chilean Communist Party and several minor left organisations. His election brought great hopes for Chile's working class. Almost exactly three years later, a military coup, led by General Pinochet, overthrew Allende's government. Allende himself died during the coup, and in the years that followed right-wing military forces murdered, tortured and imprisoned thousands of working class activists. Pinochet's government turned Chile into a neoliberal laboratory, which further impoverished the Chilean people.

Fifty years later Allende is often celebrated as a pioneer of peaceful socialist change. In April 2019 the US socialist journal *Jacobin* published an article titled *What Bernie Sanders and His Supporters Can Learn from Salvador Allende.* Aimed at the thousands of activists around Sanders' presidential campaign, its author Ben Beckett said that Allende "enacted a political revolution in Chile... it also came closest to developing a successful democratic socialist revolution".[155]

However, this is a dangerous argument. The tragic end to Allende's government is a lesson in the dangers that socialists face if they fail to challenge the capitalist state. Allende's approach—which constantly undermined workers' struggle and power to appease the capitalists—shows what can happen if left-wing politicians seek to enact reforms to capitalism without taking on the system itself.

So what actually happened between 1970 and 1973? Allende's election took place following a period of intense class struggle. On assuming office, he began to introduce a series of reforms. The reforms themselves were limited, but what frightened Chile's capitalists was not the content—but the context of growing class struggle and workers' confidence.[156] UP itself was far from revolutionary, in fact it had "displayed an unerring commitment to electoral alliances".[157]

Allende was careful to make his intentions clear. The month after the election he had signed a "Statute of Constitutional Guarantee" which made it clear that his government would "respect the state and its structures and leave intact all those instruments which the bourgeoisie had evolved to defend its class interests—the education system, the Church, the mass media and the armed forces". [158] Allende's economic programme was limited, with a plan to nationalise just 150 of 3,500 firms.

Allende envisaged the UP government working closely with existing capitalist interests to develop a "mixed economy". Beckett writes of Allende that he "spent much of his time in office in a balancing act, trying to build workers' power and self-confidence while not provoking capitalists into attacking to a degree the Chilean working class and his government could not yet withstand".[159] This is inaccurate—in office, Allende spent most of his time placating the capitalist class, trying to hold back workers' struggle and making repeated concessions to the right.

When workers began to mobilise, the Allende government stepped back, refusing to be involved and, on occasion, allowed the use of troops to repress protests and strikes. Mike Gonzalez explains the contradictions that arose in Chile as workers and peasants took the opportunity of the new government to begin demanding change:

> While UP undoubtedly retained political hegemony

> within the working-class movement, the struggle itself posed political questions that could not be answered within the framework of the UP's reformism. If the workers' and peasants' organisations were demobilised because they lay outside UP control, what guarantees could the government offer in return that the right to protest and demonstrate would not be curtailed by the police or threatened by armed right-wing groups? Would Allende take on the factory owners and stop them closing or sabotaging their plants if the workers; themselves did not do it?[160]

For the Chilean working class these were concrete questions. The Chilean bosses were trying to provoke a crisis by closing factories, shops and businesses down. A key event came in October 1972 when the bosses of the lorry companies shut down the main transportation systems. The absence of an adequate rail network in Chile meant that the economy was highly dependent on road haulage to move goods. In response to these provocations workers' organisations responded by taking over factories and workplaces, reopening shops and organising the distribution of goods.

As workers' resisted the bosses' offensive, their organising began to open up much wider possibilities for social change. By reopening companies and running factories, workers' were raising the possibility of workers' control of the economy. This was what terrified the Chilean capitalist class.

Workers' themselves began to think beyond the limited reforms offered by Allende. Gonzalez quotes a group of workers:

> The bosses aren't going to tell us what to do... So we opened the stores, took out the raw materials, and just kept on production—production didn't stop here for a single moment... You can see people working with real joy. I think we've realised in these last few days that what we're defending is something more than just a

plate of beans.[161]

Marian Schlotterbeck has written about the fundamental changes happening in Chile at the time:

> [P]eople stood up to the boss for the first time, people organized their neighbours and collectively carried out an action to occupy land and started building their homes and building a new community. These are really radical transformations in the ways in which people conceive of themselves, in the ways in which they conceive of their place in society.
>
> What happened in Chile was what I call "everyday revolutions"—transformations in how people saw their place in society, and saw an opening to act... But as people came together to try to transform their daily realities, those transformations challenged the status quo, challenged the de facto powers that had been held by the traditional landed elite in Chile. And so they were a threat to the status quo—they were claiming a life with greater dignity, a life in which they felt like equals in society.[162]

This was precisely what the ruling class feared.

Despite the instincts of such workers, no one on the left was articulating any strategy that could develop and strengthen these movements. Even the far left was disorganised, and tended to direct its polemic at Allende's government. Nonetheless workers' action did protect Allende's government, but he responded by telling workers to "return to work and restore the factories to their owners".[163]

By 1973, the right was openly talking about a coup against Allende. Allende, for his part, "now led a coalition which no longer functioned as a political leadership... [and] he embarked on one set of discussions after another with the right-wing parties".[164]

But in Chile in 1972-1973 there was a potential alternative. The networks of workers, student, squatters and activists that had come together to resist the bosses' offensive had formed coordinating assemblies, called cordones. These bodies demonstrated that there was the possibility of an alternative power evolving out of workers' struggle, which could stand up to the bosses. Unfortunately, the movement took only the most tentative steps towards this goal.

In contrast, the right was more confident and better organised. Many workers expected a coup, but had little concept of the scale of the violence to come.[165] Allende's strategy of placating the bosses meant he saw the military as an ally, not a threat. Indeed, he had actually used the military against some workers' strikes and brought generals into his cabinet. In June 1973 when Colonel Souper attempted a coup, the cordones mobilised to stop it, but Allende turned to the military for help.

Gonzalez explains what happened next:

> The leadership of the military opposed only the timing of Souper's action... As far as these circles were concerned, the response of the working class to Souper's action tipped the balance away from a political solution. In the armed forces, the mass reaction provoked urgent discussion about the need for military intervention.[166]

In the aftermath workers' confidence grew to the extent that most "functions of production, distribution, workers' defence and social services" were organised by workers.[167] Rather than develop this power to strengthen his position and that of the workers, Allende blamed the left for the slide toward civil war. As a result, the workers' movement was fatally undermined.

On 11 September 1973, when tanks surrounded Allende's residence, there was almost no resistance from the workers' movement. The military immediately began rounding up activists and herding them towards an improvised prison camp in the National Football Stadium. Over the next days and weeks, thousands were tortured and murdered.

It has become commonplace to blame General Pinochet's coup on the US government and the CIA. While there is strong evidence of CIA involvement, to understand Allende's fate we need to see how the Chilean capitalist class organised against the threat to it. As Brazilian Marxist Emir Sader has noted, UP:

> ...did not analyse what would be the real conditions for defeating the existing power and building an alternative one. It believed that these would emerge through the application of a programme of essentially economic reforms, as a natural consequence, and ended up falling into an economism that left it incapable of taking on other decisive centres of power, like the Armed Forces, imperialism and the private press.[168]

Rather than challenging the capitalist state and seeking to replace it with a workers' state that could wield power against the capitalists, Allende's Popular Unity government "found itself smothered with the state apparatus and eventually defeated by a military coup supported by all of the bourgeoisie."[169]

These lessons are crucial today. It is not hard to imagine a contemporary, green-left government elected to power promising to enact reforms to tackle climate and social injustice. It is also not hard to imagine that, without a powerful movement prepared to take on the capitalist state, the big corporations, the entrenched fossil fuel interests and the right wing will mobilise to undermine that government. What sort of movement do we need to take on the capitalist state? The next two chapters will begin to answer this crucial question.

Chapter 6
Changing the world: What sort of movement do we need?

In 2019, just before the Covid pandemic, a global revolt shook ruling classes in Hong Kong, Colombia, Chile, Haiti, Catalonia, Algeria, Sudan, Lebanon and Iraq.[170] Protest movements in Britain were not on the scale of those in other countries though 2019 saw large, inspiring climate strikes and Extinction Rebellion (XR) demonstrations involving tens of thousands, which caused major disruption. Since then, despite the limitations imposed by Covid lockdowns we have seen mass protests, particularly the Black Lives Matter movement which returned to the streets in enormous numbers in May 2020 following the murder of George Floyd.[171]

Such movements are inspirational. In fact, they are the hope for the future. Activists must celebrate these protests, and do everything we can to re-establish them following the interruption caused by the pandemic. However, socialists argue it is not enough just to build social movements. We must build the sort of movements that can win fundamental change. This requires thinking about a strategy to take on the system. How should we organise? What social forces do we need to mobilise in order to win? Can small groups substitute for mass action?

Big strategic debates like these happen in all social movements. In recent movements, activists are also raising wider question—about the role of the police, political and organisational leadership, the role of the working class and the role of violence versus non-violence. Anyone who has been involved in Extinction Rebellion will remember intense discussions about violence, the role of the police and racism. Similar discussions are happening in different contexts in movements around the world

These debates are crucial ones for activists—it is no exaggeration to argue that the fate of humanity hangs on them. In this chapter, I want to outline a revolutionary socialist strategy for building a movement that can fight for climate and social justice in the face of the capitalist state. This will mean critically engaging with the ideas of some leading activists, though I emphasise this is very much in the sense of wanting to work together with others to change the world.

I will start with a series of arguments made by environmental activist Roger Hallam in Britain. Hallam was one of the founding members of XR, and a key theoretical figure in the movement. He was effectively suspended from XR because of an interview he gave relativising the Holocaust, but continues to be active in the environmental movement. His argument remains the main statement of the XR's strategy, but raises important questions for the wider movement about how social change can be successful. Hallam puts forward an argument for disruptive direct action:

> We have to be clear. Conventional campaigning does not work. Sending emails, giving money to NGOs, going on A-to-B marches. Many wonderful people have dedicated years of their lives to all this, but it's time to be honest. Conventional campaigning has failed to bring about the necessary change. Emissions have increased by 60 percent since 1990 and they are still going up, increasing by 2.7 percent in 2019 alone.
>
> Looking at that 30 years of appalling failure, the reason is clear. The rich and powerful are making too much money from our present suicidal course. You

> cannot overcome such entrenched power by persuasion and information. You can only do it by disruption.

Hallam then argues that there are two types of disruption. The first is violence:

> Violence is a traditional method. It is brilliant at getting attention and creating chaos and disruption, but it is often disastrous when it comes to creating progressive change. Violence destroys democracy and the relationships with opponents, which are vital to creating peaceful outcomes to social conflict. The social science is totally clear on this: violence does not optimise the chance of successful, progressive outcomes. In fact, it almost always leads to fascism and authoritarianism.[172]

In contrast Hallam argues that the alternative, second type of disruption, non-violence, is shown by "all the studies" to be more successful.[173] Here Hallam is arguing that almost all the tactics of the left and progressive movements of the previous decades are inadequate.

In contrast to this, other activists have argued for militant action that is not afraid of using violence against fossil fuel capitalism. In 2021 Swedish Marxist Andreas Malm published his provocatively titled, and widely read book, *How to Blow Up a Pipeline*.[174] In it, he rages against the inaction of governments on climate change and the failure of the environmental movement to win more from international governments despite years of protests outside COP conferences and impressive mobilisations, including many militant actions that Malm has been part of himself.

Malm points out that the capitalists will not dismantle the fossil fuel system themselves:

> It takes a lot of capital to get something like a deep-water field to pump up the black gold, and some time

> must pass before the initial investment pays off, and once profits have come gushing in, the owner will have an abiding interest in keeping the unit at work for as long as possible.[175]

Therefore, Malm proposes mass, direct action that violently targets infrastructure:

> So here is what this movement of millions should do, for a start: announce and enforce the prohibition [on all new CO_2-emitting devices]. Damage and destroy new CO_2-emitting devices. Put them out of commission, pick them apart, demolish them, burn them, blow them up. Let the capitalists who keep on investing in the fire know that their properties will be trashed... if we can't get a prohibition, we can impose a de facto one with our bodies and any other means.[176]

Malm puts a different spin on Hallam's argument. While Malm rejects the non-violent approach supported by many in Extinction Rebellion, and he argues for a mass movement—he too believes that many of the campaigning strategies used in the past are inadequate.

How do socialists respond to these debates? Firstly, socialists are in favour of mass movements—we want to see the biggest number of people involved in protests, demonstrations, meetings and strikes. Secondly, we are not pacifists in the sense that we reject all violence—at times, our movements will need to confront the forces of the state, defend themselves from attack and be disruptive. In fact, social change has always been disruptive—blocking roads, shutting workplaces with pickets and mass protests are disruptive. We also do not condemn those who destroy property—the great struggles to win the vote, won, in part because militant suffragettes broke windows and vandalised buildings as part of a wider mass movement. Thirdly, we think that the working class is the agent of change, the force with the power to stop capitalism, and we work to maximise the participation of workers in our movements.

In the rest of this chapter, I will explore what these general socialist points mean for building social movements today, and how they link to the project of replacing capitalism with a socialist society.

*

Let us begin with the question of violence and non-violence, a subject that has recently seen heated debates within movements like Extinction Rebellion and Black Lives Matter.[177] In this debate, our starting point is a hatred of violence. Capitalism is a system of violence. War is endemic to capitalism—the logical outcome of a system that pitches rival capitals against each other, dividing the world up into competing nation-states. Modern warfare also raises the possibility of nuclear conflict that would drive humanity extinct. This is violence on an enormous scale.

However, violence does not just arise from conflict—it also arises out of the structural inequalities of capitalism that on a daily basis leads to enormous suffering. Capitalism is an enormously wealthy system, where a handful of billionaires control vast amounts of wealth, yet billions of people suffer from poverty. It is a system where thousands of people die on a daily basis because they lack clean water, adequate amounts of food, proper shelter or access to medicines that could prevent disease. Even in the wealthy north, low pay, high rents and cuts to public services mean millions of people suffer regularly. However, the violence of capitalism is disproportionately felt by the population of the Global South. Colonialism and imperialism robbed them of wealth and resources, and they suffer foremost from the effects of poverty, hunger and environmental crisis.

Apologists for capitalism, those who defend the system and condemn the violence of protesters or rioters rarely turn their anger on a system that breeds hunger, poverty, inequality and rests on oppression and exploitation.

In contrast, most people become socialists because they reject violence, oppression and exploitation. However, that does not mean that socialists are pacifists. We understand that in the face of the violence of capitalism, and the potential violence of the state, we cannot simply wish violence away. At times, our movement will need to defend itself against the forces of repression. We also argue that people have the right to self-defence—whether it is a victim of racism fighting back against a far-right thug, an anti-racism protest blocking a fascist march, or a group of strikers resisting a police attack.

Socialists do not define our movements by the question of violence. Instead, we argue that change comes from mass action by social movements which challenge institutions, governments and the system itself. We understand that at different times, different tactics will be required. We hope to avoid violence, but do not reject it out of hand, because we understand that our opponents will resort to violence if they think they need it.

At the same time though, socialists think that our biggest strength and our greatest defence against violence is a mass movement which can shut down our opponents. Building such movements requires mobilising working people in large numbers.

The working class

Socialists see the working class as the force for change in society. This is not simply because workers are numerically larger than any other group in society, though that is important. It is because through their role in society, workers have enormous power.

Earlier in this book, we looked at the way that working people are central to capitalist production. The capitalists extract surplus value from workers, which is the basis for their profits. A worker in a factory making products creates more value than they are paid. Even if workers are not involved directly in manufacturing, they are essential to the functioning of the whole system. Workers in call centres, IT, distribution hubs, offices, agriculture, mining and so on create surplus value for the capitalists. Public sector workers in healthcare are essential in making sure the wider workforce is fit and healthy, transport workers help people get to work on time, and teachers ensure that young people are educated enough to go to work.

*

In Britain, we are frequently told that the working class has lost its power in the transition to a "weightless" economy based on the service industry and technology. The suggestion is that because of a decline in manufacturing, traditionally powerful groups of workers—such as those in mining, steel, coal and factories—have disappeared and the working class cannot fight back. Yet a closer look at the figures shows a complex picture, which challenges this analysis. In her recent book Jane Hardy describes a more complex situation of long-term decline in manufacturing, but at the same time points out the blurred "demarcation between producing goods and services" which means "real production still matters for British capitalism". She quotes figures that demonstrate the sheer size of the British working class, with over 33 million workers in Britain in 2020, of whom almost 3 million are in manufacturing, over 2 million in construction and so on. Public sectors such as health and social work and education employ significant numbers of people (4.5 million and 3.5 million respectively), but the private sector still employs 25.7 million people, 78 percent of the total.[78]

It is important to point out that all these workers have economic power—they are all part of the capitalist system—and when they strike, they restrict the ability of the bosses to make profit. Strikes by health and education workers cause massive disruption to the system, and if we learnt one thing from the pandemic, it is that workers such as cleaners, drivers, delivery workers, technicians and so on, play crucial roles in making sure the whole economy functions.

Hardy also points to some myths about the traditional "industrial" working class. For instance, in Britain, "manufacturing has never constituted an absolute majority of the work force"; the sector peaked at 40 percent in in 1911. While technological development means the production of goods needs fewer workers—this also means that smaller numbers of workers have more power. [179] The effort that multinationals like Amazon or Starbucks put into stopping trade union organisation drives shows that they are fearful of workers' power. Hardy argues that the narrative of industrial decline hides a more complex story whereby workers retain power because of the changed nature of British capitalism:

> Pronouncements of the death of Britain's manufacturing sector ignore the existence of strong pockets of activity where their economic importance is disproportionately greater than the amount of employment generated. The statistics supporting the story of industrial decline underestimate the continuing importance of manufacturing by taking a narrow view of the chain of activities that result in the production of tangible goods and the way that surplus value is dispersed throughout this chain.[180]

Recent years have seen some academics suggest that "precarious jobs"—workers on short-term contracts, zero-hours or temporary contracts—mean it is harder to fight back. There is, of course, some truth to this. However, as Hardy points out, the reality is that all jobs are "precarious under capitalism" because the system is constantly changing—destroying old industries and creating new ones.[181] In fact, some of the very industries that became closely associated with powerful trade unions, excellent pay and conditions and life-long jobs, used to be considered precarious. Dock workers in the 19th century, for instance, were considered to have low-skilled, temporary work and impossible to organise—yet by the 20th century they formed some of the most powerful sections of the British labour movement. Similarly, the building industry—notorious for dangerous conditions, temporary contracts and easy hiring and firing—saw a massive wave of struggle in the 1970s including a national strike in 1972 that eventually won an impressive national pay deal.[182]

Key to establishing decent pay, conditions and contracts is not working in a specific industry—it is class struggle. Agricultural workers in the 1870s worked long-hours in isolated conditions, yet an initiative to form a trade union in Warwickshire in 1872 quickly saw a national union grow out of a major strike wave, winning significant pay rises for workers. Employers eventually rolled back these gains amid a decline in struggle and economic crisis, but they would never have been won without strikes.

Today strikes and union drives among cleaners, delivery drivers and Amazon workers continue to show that so-called precarious workers are part of a working class and can fight and organise.

Joseph Choonara sums up the strength of the world's workers:

> Around 1.8 billion people now engage in wage labour, an increase of 600 million since 2000. Not only is the working class vast, it is also more concentrated in towns and cities than ever before. The urban share of the global population has, since 2000, risen from 47 percent to 56 percent—an extra 1.4 billion people live in urban settings compared to two decades ago. The combination of urbanisation and proletarianisation is reflected in many of the countries in the current cycle of revolt. Chile's urban labour force rose from 3.7 million in 1990 to 7.3 million last year, Ecuador's from 3.3 million in 2000 to 5.1 million in 2018.[183]

Today, the global working class is larger than it has ever been. The world's economy is more integrated than ever. The decline of manufacturing in the industrial north means that workers in the Global South have enormous power—their action can disrupt work and economic activity globally. Just in time production, global supply chains and so on give workers enormous power—the question is whether workers will use it.

*

Workers have power under capitalism because without them the system stops. By withdrawing their labour workers have the ability to hit the profits of capitalism. Without their labour the system cannot function. That is why Marx and Engels described workers as the "gravediggers" of capitalism. Capitalism needs workers. The "condition for capital is wage-labour", said Marx and Engels in the *Communist Manifesto*, but capitalism also brings workers together in concentrations that gives them power.[184]

Workers are not separate to the environmental movement. Most people on Extinction Rebellion protests, climate strikes or the COP26 demonstrations will work for a living. However, the working class is much larger than the environmental movement. The movement must reach out to the wider working class and maximise the involvement of workers in our protests and demonstrations.

The power of organised workers is why socialists try to maximise their involvement in campaigns. Earlier we looked at the British climate jobs campaign. This is a deliberate attempt to argue that workers have a collective interest in being involved in the environmental movement—using this campaign activists are able to reach out to organised workers and the trade unions and demonstrate that environmental politics is not an abstract issue, but directly relevant to working class people. At the same time, we can point to the strategic power of workers and their ability to "stop the system" as being able to disrupt the system in a powerful way.

Will workers fight back?

Socialists argue that workers are key to bringing fundamental social change. At the same time, most workers are not revolutionary outside of revolutionary periods. This is because there is a contradiction—Marx argued that workers are the revolutionary class, but at the same time, the dominant ideas in society are those of the ruling class. The mass media, our education system, and the bosses constantly tell workers that we could not run society. They use racism, sexism and homophobia to divide us, at the same time as telling us that workers are too ignorant, too racist, sexist or homophobic to run society. Workers are told that there is no point resisting or protesting and instead, we should wait for elections to choose different politicians and at the same time the media demonises those who do speak out.

Despite society's inequality, exploitation and oppression, it is no surprise that workers do not always fight back. Strike levels in many parts of the world are very low but that does not mean there is no anger, and anger can sometimes spill over into social movements and strikes.

One reason for the low levels of strikes is confidence. The defeat of the most powerful trade union movements in Britain by Margaret Thatcher has left lasting demoralisation in sections of the trade union movement. Something similar happened in the United States around the same time when Ronald Reagan was able to defeat trade unionists, undermining workers' confidence to resist his neo-liberal policies. That being said, Thatcher did not have things her own way. We should never forget that the anti-Poll Tax movement, a mass movement of non-payment, and protest eventually forced her from office.

It is not simply a question of workers' confidence. Governments have worked to make it harder for workers' to strike. In Britain, anti-trade union legislation makes it difficult to go on strike, with trade unionists needing to get large majorities in complex official ballots before they can take action. The erosion of the shop stewards movement, the rank and file, and trade union organisers on the shop floor who could coordinate and organise resistance, has also undermined the union movement.[185]

While revolutionary socialists understand that workers'

have the power to change society, for most of the time the vast majority of workers do not recognise this. Indeed, even most socialists do not appreciate this—seeing capitalism as something that can only be reformed, rather than replaced. According to the Italian Marxist Antonio Gramsci, workers usually have "contradictory consciousness". They simultaneously hold ideas that they receive from the system itself—pro-capitalist arguments articulated in the media, taught in school or received from politicians—and ideas that contradict the capitalist story.

According to Gramsci:

> [The worker] has two theoretical consciousnesses (or one contradictory consciousness): one which is implicitly in his activity and which in reality unites him with all his fellow-workers in the practical transformation of the real world; and one, superficially explicitly or verbal, which he has inherited from the past and uncritically absorbed.[186]

In discussing Gramsci's theory, Alex Callinicos argues that "the 'means of mental production'—the education system, the mass media etc—do not so much induce in workers' as systematically false consciousness as prevent the formation of a coherent revolutionary class-consciousness".[187]

Outside of revolutionary periods, the dominant ideas in society are those of the ruling class. Nonetheless, there is a constant challenge to these ideas because of the workers' lived experience. For instance, workers might believe that immigrants are to blame for low wages, but also know that they need to stand united with workers from all different backgrounds to win a strike that can increase wages.

Key to challenging the ideas that hold workers back from developing revolutionary consciousness is struggle. In mass struggles, workers break down their old ideas very quickly. Old ideas go out the window, and new radical ones appear, seemingly out of nowhere. Remember how workers in Chile in 1973, resisting a bosses offensive, reopened workplaces and started to raise demands about workers' control of production, going far further than left politicians wanted them to?

Every strike, however small, raises wider questions about society. Even workers' who lose a strike ballot can draw lessons about how the system is stacked against them. When workers are on strike, experiencing solidarity and unity, seeing police repression and experiencing their own power to shut workplaces, they can develop new consciousness. However, none of this is automatic

Famously during the British Miners' strike of 1984-5, the involvement of LGBT+ people in the strike, in the form of Lesbians and Gays Support the Miners (LGSM), broke down homophobic attitudes. As depicted in the film *Pride* in return for solidarity from LGSM, banners from the NUM led the 1985 Pride march and helped ensure that the British Labour movement took up LGBT+ equality.

The story of LGSM during the British Miners' strike is inspirational; however, it would not have happened if a young, gay, communist activist Mark Ashton had not taken the initiative to setup LGSM. This is one reason socialist organisations are important—they can help develop networks of solidarity and challenge and breakdown stereotypes.

One reason that socialists place emphasis on mass movements and demonstrations is that they can give confidence to workers, and encourage wider action. Another reason is that collective action by workers can also break down divisions within the working class. Racist, sexist and homophobic ideas are challenged through the unity of struggle. Workers linking arms on a picket line to stop scabs breaking a strike, or joining together in a mass protest, begin to break down the barriers that capitalism sets up to divide them against each other.

When you are fighting back it is much easier to see that the real enemy is the boss attacking your wages, or a government restricting your rights, rather than immigrants, women or

LGBT+ people. The miner's strike saw pitched battles between the forces of the state and working class communities, and it saw the transformation of social attitudes among the miners. Among a workforce known for its sexist attitudes, women came to the fore in the strike, setting up solidarity organisations, speaking at meetings and protests, and leading demonstrations.

If we go back to Gramsci's twin consciousness in workers' heads, socialists want to develop and give confidence to that part of the workers' ideas that show the possibility of collective action winning. This is why socialists are in favour of mass social movements and mass protest.

Taking to the streets

On 15 February 2003 up to 10 million people took part in protests against the coming imperialist war on Iraq. In London, around 1.5 million people demonstrated, marching to an enormous rally in Hyde Park. The protests were some of the largest in history. Yet a little over a month later forces led by the US and Britain attacked Iraq. Some people in the anti-war movement drew the conclusion that such marches were a waste of time, drawing the conclusion, like Roger Hallam, that "A to B marches" do not work.

Socialists do not take that attitude. Indeed socialists were central to building the Stop the War Coalition that called the march and mobilising for the protest itself. We see mass protests as being an integral part of developing the sort of movement that can change the world.

The mass protests did have one tangible result. When later British governments wanted to attack Iran and Syria, they did not do so for fear of a renewed anti-war movement. Those who decry "A to B" marches fail to understand the importance of those marches in giving an identity to and creating a visible, confident and mass anti-war movement.

That said, socialists also argue that mass protests can give confidence to workers to take further action. In January 2003, Scottish rail workers refused to move a train carrying ammunition intended for use in Iraq. The rail workers explicitly described themselves as against the war.[188] There is little doubt that this strike action would not have happened without a mass protest movement giving encouragement to the workers. Had more workers taken action like this—refusing to work in protest against the war—the anti-war movement would have risen to a new level. Unfortunately, the anti-war movement was not able to develop more workers' action like the Scottish rail workers. More strikes against the war would have made it harder for the British government to take part in the attack on Iraq. Different wings of the movement, strike action, mass protest and direct action, can all feed off each other and give confidence—drawing new people in and encouraging further action.

On our own, we are relatively powerless. Our protests as individuals make very little difference. This is true of protest, but it is also true of wider individualised campaigns. The environmental movement has often seen calls for people to change their diets, boycott particular brands or cycle instead of driving cars. People making those choices often do so for good reasons, hoping to make a small difference. Socialists support those who make these choices—we are not moralists—but the key point is that it is not a strategy to win systemic change.

In isolation, these small changes can make little or no difference. Individual dietary changes such as avoiding meat, has no impact at all on industrial agriculture, and easily become incorporated into capitalism—with fast food giants now selling vegan products alongside sausage rolls and burgers.

Moral campaigns urging us to change our personal behaviour also do little to raise workers' consciousness about wider capitalism and their power to collectively change the world. By definition, acting as an individual isolates you from wider social forces. However, engaging in action with others always has the potential to raise wider collective responses. In the 2000s there was a trade union campaign to boycott Coca Cola because of the manufacturer's alleged links with Colombian paramilitary forces who had killed trade unionists. Individuals refusing to buy the drink were making a moral choice. But workers organising to have Coke removed from their canteens, or vending machines returned were engaging in campaigning that began from the need for a collective response.

Boycotts can make a real difference particularly when they are linked to wider, collective campaigns. In the 1980s black activists in apartheid South Africa called on people around the world to boycott the country. They asked people to stop buying South African goods, encouraged musicians and artists to refuse to perform in South Africa and demanded a boycott of companies that did business with the country. Similarly today, Palestinian activists have called for a boycott of Israel in solidarity with their movement. Such boycotts can be incredibly important in supporting the action of people on the ground—not as a substitute for such activism.

What matters is mass collective action, but this is not to say that socialists refuse to protest until there are millions on the streets. Campaigns usually begin with small numbers, and street demonstrations by small groups are one way of raising awareness of an issue, a campaign or a strike. However, socialists always seek to try to maximise participation. We do not fetishise small protests—fundamental change will be won through mass action.

Small actions that block a road might make the headlines, but they often can be alienating for the wider working class. Here I want to return to the debate raised by Malm. Rightly, he argues for a mass environmental movement, but he does not see that movement in itself as changing things. That, he argues, will require the militant shutting down (or destruction) of fossil fuel infrastructure, backed by a mass movement of millions.

Action on such a scale, Malm believes, will mean that fossil fuel multinationals will not be inclined to invest in further developments. Malm draws inspiration from Britain's suffragette movement which also used violence tactics (arson, window breaking and property damage) to highlight their cause, but crucially he says the suffragettes wanted to "twist the arm of the state"—to force them to grant the vote to women.

Here we come to Malm's main point. He argues that because oil, coal and gas infrastructure is so large, no movement could possibly destroy it on the scale needed, so "at the end of the day, it will be states that ram through the transition or no one will".[189] Malm argues the movement has to make the state deliver this.

The problem is that Malm subordinates the mass movement to the direct action of small groups. But, winning victories against fossil fuel capital will require mass action as the *primary* tactic of the movement, even if some groups within that movement do take direct action.

The most successful campaigns against fossil fuel infrastructure have involved mass protests, not groups of individuals destroying infrastructure. The movements against pipelines, fracking wells and other infrastructure—which Naomi Klein has called "Blockadia"[190]—have been most successful when they combined mass movements and direct action.

When Shell pulled out of the North Sea Cambo oil field at the end of 2021, their press release acknowledged the "economic case for investment in this project is not strong enough at this time, as well as having the potential for delays".[191]

This announcement came immediately after at least 100,000 people protested in Scotland during COP26, protests in which Cambo had figured strongly as an activist issue. The anticipated delays that worried Shell could be expected to come from environment groups gearing up to protest over Cambo in the aftermath of the summit.

The moratorium on fracking in England, announced by the Tory government in 2019, was won by a mass campaign. It combined protests at fracking sites and direct action to block vehicles with mass demonstrations. Crucially, much of the trade union movement was opposed to fracking. Activists successfully argued that there were alternatives, which would provide more jobs without resorting to dirty fossil fuels.

At its most successful, the US campaign in Standing Rock

against the Dakota Access Pipeline involved mass protests. They were led by indigenous people and supported by environmental activists, workers and even military veteran groups. The protest camp at Standing Rock had 15,000 participants at its peak. Similarly, the movement that stopped the Keystone XL pipeline involved direct action combined with mass protests, such as the tens of thousands of people who marched to the White House. Under huge pressure, then president Barack Obama blocked the plans. While Trump gave the go-ahead again, incumbent Joe Biden revoked permission on his first day in office. TC Energy, the corporation behind Keystone XL, gave up the project.

These examples show that we can stop fossil fuel expansion. But it takes mass movements combining militant tactics at specific targets, such as blockades and pickets, with mass demonstrations aimed at creating pressure on corporations and politicians. We also must be aware that stopping the Cambo oil field, winning fracking bans or stopping a pipeline may well only be temporary victories under capitalism. As I write this book, the British Tory government is using the Ukraine war as an excuse to restart the Cambo oil field project and revisit fracking. Our response must be to reawaken and rebuild the movements that stopped these projects last time, but also argue that unless capitalism is finished the fossil fuel companies will always try and return to regain lost ground.

Powerful social movements can win reforms from capitalism. We can stop fossil fuel expansion, or make governments ban fracking—indeed all the rights we have today have been won by struggles in the past. But if we do not end capitalism, then the capitalists will constantly try to revoke the gains our side has won. Reforms are not necessarily permanent. It is not enough to win a few temporary gains. We have to win permanent change.

*

The larger our movements, the more likely they are to pull in wider social forces that can be won to oppose fossil fuel corporations. This is never automatic. It requires patient argument as well as protests. For instance, winning the trade union movement to an anti-fracking position meant creating a big protest movement with demonstrations and other actions, which workers could join.

At the same time, we had to show there were alternatives that could create jobs and protect communities. I vividly remember being part of numerous trade union meetings in the North West of England in the 2010s arguing against the position that fracking would create many jobs. Given the shortage of jobs and levels of unemployment in parts of the region, there was an understandable interest in the new industry.

We had to show that investment in renewable energy programmes would create more, and better, jobs. The 2014 edition of the *One Million Climate Jobs* pamphlet included, for instance, a case study about jobs in Salford and the Fylde. This area in the North West of England was targeted by the fracking industry, but we were able to show that only 630 jobs would be created, compared to 4,500 if the Climate Jobs programme was implemented—based on renewable energy.[192] But it wasn't just about jobs—the movement also had to argue that fracking was poisonous, dangerous and drove climate change—linking the wider environmental questions to the specific economic issues.

In turn, once we had won trade unions to an anti-fracking position their participation gave confidence and solidarity to the environmental movement. It also raised questions about the potential power of workers to challenge the system.

In contrast, small groups of militant activists can be easily isolated from the wider community. In the 1990s, for instance, Earth First! was campaigning against logging, which was destroying habitats in the Pacific North West of the US. The government and timber bosses turned the debate into "jobs vs the environment".

It was common to see car bumper stickers with slogans like, 'Save a Logger, Eat an Owl'. In turn, some environmental activists lumped workers together with the bosses. They failed to find common ground with workers who had the potential to be a significant force fighting for jobs and the environment.

Importantly though, while socialists might be critical of tactics like those of Earth First! or the Insulate Britain protests, we don't denounce them and we certainly do not side with the state or with the right against them. In 2022, when Insulate Britain were given heavy sentences for blocking motorways in protest at government inaction over climate change, socialists sided with the protesters, while simultaneously arguing that militant action needed to be part of a mass movement if it was to be effective. Right-wing politicians or newspapers that attacked Insulate Britain for inconveniencing people commuting to work are demonstrating the grossest hypocrisy. They have nothing to say about climate change, or even about the cuts to public transport that have made commuting such a nightmare for workers.

The repression used against Insulate Britain protesters and others who have tried to shut down buildings and roads in protests deserve our support because of the draconian punishments handed out by the British courts. In March 2021 Ryan Roberts was given a 14-year sentence after his involvement in a Kill the Bill protest in Bristol in March 2021.

Capitalist states have never been afraid of using violence and the threat of heavy custodial sentences to protect the profits of business. And tragically it has frequently been the fossil fuel industry that has benefited from such capitalist support.

We need only remember the Ogoni Nine, a group of indigenous environmental activists executed by the Nigerian state in 1995. They had been fighting the destruction of their homeland by Shell.

The ability of the capitalist state to unleash repression against individuals who are confronting the system is the biggest barrier to a strategy that relies on small group action or explicitly targets infrastructure. It is one that relies on groups of people—no matter how large they are—to try to stop the fossil fuel industry solely by targeting their infrastructure. The answer to this is not unleashing more violence from our side, but building the mass movements that can stop the functioning of capitalism itself.

We have already seen several examples in this book where physical confrontation by mass protests has won victories—as in the example of the Battle of Saltley Gate in 1972. Indeed, these sorts of movements are close to what Malm is calling for. However, within these movements the militant action was part of the wider mass action. It would be a disaster if mass movements were simply used as a passive stage army subordinated to the brave, substitutionist actions of a minority engaged in violent direct action.

We must be wary of seeing action by small groups of individuals, however brave they are, as being more radical than mass action. In fact, the most radical action possible is workers going on strike precisely because it hits profits and is a direct challenge to the system. In doing this, workers are raising the potential for alternative forms of power.

*

Malm concludes by saying "it will be states that ram through the transition or no one will". This begs the question "what sort of state?" The capitalist state is based on the potential use of organised violence to protect the status quo and we see that in action every time a protester is beaten, arrested or incarcerated for blocking the entrance to a refinery. A capitalist state will not be "shaken" out of "business as usual" by a mass movement, even one using mass sabotage.[102] The only state that would do this is one that is organised in the interest of the vast majority of people—those whose collective interest is stopping the destruction of the environment, and repressing the class whose interests are those of the fossil fuel corporations.

That type of state is a workers' state, and it can only come about through a mass revolutionary movement that overthrows the capitalist state. In this chapter, we have discussed how social movements can win. Socialists want to go further. We want to build a movement that can win fundamental change by getting rid of capitalism itself.

Revolutions, as we saw earlier in this book, have occurred numerous times in capitalism's history. In the next chapter, we will look at four inspiring examples of revolution. In all of these cases, ordinary women and men have fought to change the world. The stories of how they did this, can inspire us today but they also have important lessons for those resisting today.

Chapter 7
Revolutionary lessons

Capitalism began in Western Europe in the 17th century, rapidly spreading around the world. Revolutions, such as the English and French Revolutions, saw the replacement of the old feudal order with societies that allowed the unfettered development of capitalism to take place. These were often violent affairs, which saw the old ruling class overthrown and defeated and a new state take the place of the previous order. In these cases, a rising capitalist class, the bourgeoisie, was able to mobilise forces from below—including sections of the old aristocracy, the rural gentry but, crucially, the merchant and "middling" classes. These latter groups' economic interests were linked to new forms of capital accumulation—which were held back by the old feudal order and came into constant conflict with it. The ability of the bourgeoisie to overthrow feudalism needed mass pressure from below to defeat the old aristocratic order and end feudal rule.

But the spread of capitalism around the world did not always take place via revolution from below. For instance, the Meiji Revolution in Japan in the 1860s saw a "revolution from above" abolish the old feudal lords and install a new bourgeois government.[194] In other cases, Europeans, and then other emergent capitalist powers such as the US, imposed new capitalist social organisation on colonies in the Global South.

This revolutionary transformation of society created a capitalist social order, where bourgeois nation-states competed in a global market to maximise the profits of their own capitalist classes. Over time, just as feudal society became a "fetter" on the development of new social organisation, and forced the bourgeoisie into conflict with it, capitalism has become a fetter on the further development, or even survival, of human society. Capitalism must itself be overthrown.

However, a key argument of this book has been that a transition from capitalism to socialism, cannot take place from above—nor can it come through reforming the system. It must come out of a mass, revolutionary movement from below that overthrows the capitalist state and replaces it with a workers' state through the creation of alternative organisations of workers power. What would these revolutions look like? History offers us many clues.

Firstly, we need to distinguish between political and social revolutions. Political revolutions are those that see a change within the existing system, without a corresponding change to the social and economic system. Political revolution might mean the fall of a particular dictator, regime or government. In 2011, revolutions in Tunisia and Egypt saw the fall of the dictators Ben Ali and Mubarak. The protesters and strikers who overthrew these dictators wanted thoroughgoing change in particular the end of military rule in Egypt. However, at the start of those revolutions only a few saw that the process could go further and lead to fundamental social change in society by overthrowing capitalism.

In contrast, a social revolution sees a fundamental change to the economic order. For instance, the French Revolution of 1789 overthrew the French monarchy, an absolutist feudal system in favour of a bourgeois system of government and the emergence of a capitalist mode of production. As we will see, the Russian Revolution of October 1917 saw the overthrow of a capitalist society and the creation of a society based on workers' power.

Political revolution can lead to social revolution. The overthrow of a particular dictator might lead to the military trying to hold onto power, which could force the revolutionary movement to create organisations of workers' power to coordinate and organise their resistance. These institutions then could form the basis for more fundamental social change. Workers' anger at economic hardship and lack of democracy might lead to them overthrowing a repressive government, but when those workers realise that parliamentary democracy doesn't solve problems like low pay their revolution may begin to go further. In both these cases, a political revolution can move into a social revolution.

Revolution is a reality for capitalism. The very nature of capitalist society where a minority ruling class exploits the masses in a system prone to periodic economic crisis means that resistance and revolution are an inevitability. Understanding historic dynamics of revolutionary events can help illuminate what revolution means today. Though we must be cautious—history never repeats itself exactly. Revolutions arise out of concrete historical circumstances and their paths are shaped by the political and economic reality of their time.

The rest of this chapter will look at four examples. As each section will show, I intend these particular examples to draw out lessons for socialists organising today. These examples show how workers' power is key to pushing revolutions forward, how mass movements break down divisions in society and lift up oppressed groups, while giving workers' confidence to organise and lead in ways they never would have thought possible just days before the revolutions began. But they also show that for revolutions to succeed they need to navigate complex political situations as they unfold, and crucial to doing this successfully is the role of organised revolutionaries in political parties. Tragically, as we shall see, only in the Russian Revolution, was there a party large enough, with clear revolutionary objectives, that could lead the revolution to success.

Finally, in these examples I have tried to show how revolutions bring out the capacity for workers' self-organisation. Without workers organising, revolutions would be impossible—workers' come together to plan strikes and occupations, discuss politics and tactics and coordinate action. But in revolutionary periods this organisation can go further and create the institutions that can become the basis for a new society, organised from the bottom up, by the workers themselves.

So these accounts prefigure the final chapters, which look at how a society that arises out of the revolutionary destruction of capitalism might be organised, and how it might come about.

Paris Commune 1871

> It is time people understood the true meaning of this Revolution; and this can be summed up in a few words. It meant the government of the people by the people. It was the first attempt of the proletariat to govern itself. The workers of Paris expressed this when… they declared they "understood it was their imperious duty and their absolute right to render themselves masters of their own destinies by seizing upon the governmental power.
>
> Eleanor Marx, 1886.[195]

In March 1871 the people of Paris rose up and declared the Paris Commune. In its brief period of existence, its participants demonstrated that a radical democratic society was possible. For just over two months, the workers of Paris ruled the city. They elected representatives who were paid the average wage of a worker, and who were directly accountable to those who elected them through immediate recall. The workers also organised the physical defence of their city and their revolution. Their government began introducing policies designed to dramatically address crippling poverty and transform social relations. In its brief existence, the Commune inspired radicals around the world and terrified the ruling class. Karl Marx captured this well:

> When the Paris Commune took the management of the revolution in its own hands; when plain working men

> for the first time dared to infringe upon the governmental privilege of their "natural superiors", and, under circumstances of unexampled difficulty, performed it at salaries the highest of which barely amounted to one-fifth of what, according to high scientific authority, is the minimum required for a secretary to a certain metropolitan school-board,—the old world writhed in convulsions of rage at the sight of the Red Flag, the symbol of the Republic of Labour, floating over the Hôtel de Ville.[196]

The Commune inspired many revolutionaries but for Marx and Engels the actions of the Parisian workers helped develop their understanding of revolutionary change. In particular, the experience of the Commune showed that workers could not seize, ready made, the capitalist state and use it for their own purposes. Instead, workers had to "smash" the old state apart and create a new workers' state. For Marx and Engels the Paris Commune was an example of a new workers' state—and they set about drawing out the lessons for workers' around the world.

*

The Paris Commune had its origins in the Franco-Prussian War of 1870-1871. The war saw a major defeat for France at the Battle of Sedan in September 1870. When Paris learnt of this defeat, it exploded in revolution.[197] The Government of National Defence that arose out of this revolution was in no way friendly to the ordinary people of France and its failure to organise the defence of Paris against the Prussians increased antagonism with the lower orders. Prussia's four-month siege caused appalling deprivation in Paris. The idea of wartime "national unity" was shown to be a lie as the working people of Paris suffered far worse than the rich. Food riots, unemployment and protests grew through the siege.

On 18 March 1871 the French government, led by Adolphe

Thiers, tried to disarm the predominately working class National Guard. Working class women, men and children organised to protect hundreds of cannon that Thier's wanted to confiscate. The resistance of the Parisian masses began the Paris Commune. They built barricades and encouraged government troops to revolt against their officers. To protect his forces Thiers evacuated the government and its remaining loyal troops to Versailles, the historic seat of the French monarchy, where they consolidated their strength and waited for the opportunity for revenge. The events of 18 March were a spontaneous response to the French government's attempts to disarm the revolution, but the Commune was "shaped and driven forward by individuals and organisations steeped in experience of the labour and socialist movements".[198]

The people of Paris began to construct their own state. Who were they? Historian John Merriman explains that the average Communards were young men, most of whom were born outside Paris, but had come there looking for work. The majority were "drawn from the world of Parisian work... skilled and semi-skilled workers, many working with wood, shoes, printing or small-scale metal production, and construction workers, as well as day-labourers and domestic servants". There were also shopkeepers and clerks. Female Communards were also workers "particularly [in the] textile and clothing trades".[199]

In the immediate aftermath of the 18 March revolution, leadership in the city lay in the hands of the Central Committee of the National Guard. This body called for elections to the Commune, which took place on 26 March, and saw mass participation from ordinary people from the different areas, called arrondissements, of the city. Each arrondissement elected a group of people to represent them in the Commune's leadership. One leading figure in the Commune Édouard Vaillant explained that the elected Commune was a "deliberative assembly without sufficient cohesion, whose decisiveness wasn't on a par with its good will and intentions".[200]

Such criticism was not uncommon at the time. However,

had the Commune lasted longer the struggle would likely have sharpened the leadership's politics—and seen other revolutionary workers rise to leading roles. This is because a key strength of the Commune's leadership was that it was based on accountable democracy. Arrondissements could immediately recall their elected delegates and each delegate was paid a maximum of 6,000 francs, the same as other workers. Election to the Commune was not a career, or a path to riches, it was a way to serve the working class community that elected you. This very point inspired Russian revolutionary Vladimir Lenin, who wrote during the 1917 Revolution that, "the reduction of the pay for all servants of the state to the level of 'a workman's wages'" was particularly noteworthy for it showed "the break between bourgeois democracy and proletarian democracy, between the democracy of the oppressors and the democracy of the oppressed classes".[201]

In addition to this radical experiment in democracy, the Commune legislated some remarkable changes. At the heart of these decisions was the question of private property. For the rich the concept of private property was inviolate. For the Commune, which was trying to feed, house and employ hundreds of thousands of impoverished war-weary workers, the opposite was true. The Commune decreed that lodgers could not be evicted and that debts incurred for rent during the siege were annulled. Workers could take over their enterprise if the owner had fled.

During the Prussian siege, thousands of workers had pawned their belongings, so the Commune declared that these must be returned. Other decrees saw the banning of night time work in bakeries, and pensions paid to the dependents of those killed fighting to defend the Commune, whether or not they were married, and even for illegitimate children.

These decisions showed that the Commune was beginning to organise on a very different basis to existing French society. Among the leadership, there was "at a deep level, a remarkable unanimity around the idea of the Commune as bringing social equality, justice and workers' emancipation through breaking the capitalist state".[202]

This was also seen among ordinary people. The revolution of 18 May put the working class in control of Paris, but it also transformed the people who made it. There was a thirst for ideas. Workers devoured the huge numbers of newspapers, posters, and pamphlets, produced during the Commune. On the other hand, the Commune shut down counter-revolutionary newspapers to prevent them undermining the revolution.[203]

The Commune encouraged art and artists, 400 of whom "elected a committee of forty-seven members drawn from painting, sculpture, architecture, lithography and the industrial arts". [204] Museums and art-galleries were reopened, as was the national library. Thiers' house was burnt to the ground, but not before the removal of the artistic treasures inside to galleries for the people to enjoy. Some reports say that crime dropped dramatically during the Commune, Communard Lissagaray for instance, declared in his history of the Commune that "since Paris has (had) her own police crime has disappeared", though others suggest otherwise.[205] What is important is that the workers' state was policing itself.

Women fought on the front lines for the Commune and began to demand equality and wider participation. Judy Cox writes that the Commune, "challenged hierarchies of gender which had been deeply entrenched for centuries". [206] Some historians argue that because women could not vote in the Commune elections, the Commune did not take seriously the question of women's equality. However, this ignores the radical traditions within the Commune, and the movements that led up to it, which were raising women's emancipation. Nonetheless, the fact women could not vote was a significant problem. Understanding why this was illuminates a revolutionary dynamic. Revolutions take place in the context of the society which precedes them. As Cox explained:

> The inheritences of the past shaped the formal structures of the Commune, even while the mass movement was

> establishing new priorities and aspirations. One such inheritance was the voting system used under the Second Empire that excluded women and reflected the entrenched nature of sexism in French society.[207]

Cox goes on to show that women Communards and some of the revolutionaries at the Commune's heart challenged this sexism. She singles out the "Marxist wing of the First International... the only political organisation in France which supported the female franchise".[208] The Commune itself placed women in leading positions and set itself the task of changing the sexist norms of French society.

On 8 April 1871, the Union des Femmes was founded, calling on women to "form branches in each arrondissement... it set up committees... as recruiting centres for volunteers for nursing and canteen work and barricade construction". It also demanded equal pay for women working in the Commune's factories.[209] One leader of the Commune, Arthur Arnould explained that the decree passed on pensions for the dependents of those killed in the fighting had a major significance:

> The Commune did more for the emancipation of women, for their dignity, than any of the moralists and legislators of the past... This was perhaps one of the most audacious acts... for it radically cut through a moral question and set a landmark for a profound modification of the current constitution of the family.... [It] puts a woman legally and morally on an absolutely equal footing with a man, placing things in a real moral position and striking a mortal blow against the religio-monarchic institution of marriage... The union of man and woman must be an act that is essentially free, accomplished by two responsible persons. In this union, the rights like the duties must be reciprocal and equal.[210]

The Commune also challenged organised religion, separating

the church from the state, replacing religious marriage with civil marriage and re-establishing, and simplifying divorce—all that was required was a written declaration by both partners. [211]

Cox points out that in its brief existence the Commune could not "completely uproot centuries of women's oppression", but did "promote women to positions of authority and enable women to have real power over their lives". In this regard, the revolutionary Paris Commune was far in advance of any other so-called democratic power in the world. It did this at a time when almost nowhere else in the world gave women the vote. Following the defeat of the Commune, women did not serve in French government until 1936—and could not actually vote until 1945.[212]

*

The Paris Commune was born out of revolution, but it was not born fully formed. During the Commune's 72 days, intense debates took place about how it should be organised. Its "leading bodies... were in constant flux". On the 28 April a five person-strong leadership body, the Committee of Public Safety was proposed and elected with extensive powers, which "reflected widespread frustration" with the existing setup. At heart, these frustrations reflected different arguments about how to fight the counter-revolutionary forces at Versailles, as well as wider debates about the type of democracy that should prevail in the Commune. Tragically, Thiers' invasion of Paris and the suppression of the Communards cut short these discussions.[213]

Nevertheless, what the Commune did achieve demonstrated how a new society could be born out of the smashing of the old order. Outside of the Commune itself, Marx was one of the first to grasp the significance of how the Commune organised itself:

> The Commune was formed of the municipal councillors, chosen by universal suffrage in the various wards of the town, responsible and revocable at short terms. The

> majority of its members were naturally working men, or acknowledged representatives of the working class. The Commune was to be a working, not a parliamentary body, executive and legislative at the same time.[214]

This was a radically new form of democracy. Rather than elections happening every few years, they would take place as was needed, based on mass participation and with those elected directly accountable. The Commune merged parliament and the state, its elected representatives did not simply debate - they enacted their decisions. Under capitalism hidden, unaccountable civil servants and officials enact parliamentary policy. Under the Commune it was out in the open and accountable—and those responsible could be recalled at will. In the Commune, Marx said:

> The judicial functionaries were to be divested of that sham independence which had but served to mask their abject subserviency to all succeeding governments to which, in turn, they had taken, and broken, the oaths of allegiance. Like the rest of public servants, magistrates and judges were to be elective, responsible, and revocable.[215]

The Commune could not have survived in isolation. Its participants hoped it would spread elsewhere, and indeed short-lived Communes did spring up in Lyons, Saint Etienne, Creuzot, Marseilles, Toulouse and Narbonne though none of them lasted long, or had significant participation. [216] In part this reflected the lack of development of the proletariat in these smaller towns, the lack of a large radical left outside the capital and, most significantly, the generalised experience of the siege and the defeat. The Communards certainly hoped that the Commune would spread as an organisational form across the whole country. Marx explains how it was supposed to work:

> The communal regime once established in Paris and

the secondary centres, the old centralized government would in the provinces, too, have to give way to the self-government of the producers.

In a rough sketch of national organisation, which the Commune had no time to develop, it states clearly that the Commune was to be the political form of even the smallest country hamlet, and that in the rural districts the standing army was to be replaced by a national militia, with an extremely short term of service. The rural communities of every district were to administer their common affairs by an assembly of delegates in the central town, and these district assemblies were again to send deputies to the National Delegation in Paris, each delegate to be at any time revocable and bound by the *mandat impératif* (formal instructions) of his constituents. The few but important functions which would still remain for a central government were not to be suppressed, as has been intentionally misstated, but were to be discharged by Communal and thereafter responsible agents.

The unity of the nation was not to be broken, but, on the contrary, to be organised by Communal Constitution, and to become a reality by the destruction of the state power which claimed to be the embodiment of that unity independent of, and superior to, the nation itself, from which it was but a parasitic excrescence.[217]

This was the dream of the Commune, and Marx saw in it the basis for a new form of society, based on the active participation of ordinary people. Crucially though Marx learnt from the Commune that the old capitalist state could not be taken over, it had to be smashed and replaced, as he said, "the working class cannot simply lay hold of the ready-made state machinery, and wield it for its own purposes."[218]

It was precisely because the Commune was the harbinger of a new world that the capitalist class wanted it destroyed and those who made it eliminated. On 21 May 1871, Thiers' troops entered Paris. Ordinary Parisians, men, women and even children, fought back against unbelievable odds, "street by street, house by house, and rather than surrender, burned them".[219]

The counter-revolutionary army did not simply fight to recapture Paris. It fought to destroy every trace of the revolution. Thousands of Parisians were summarily shot, tortured, raped and imprisoned in horrific conditions. The revolution of 18 March had been a revolt of the poor against the rich and this was the capitalist's revenge. Lissagaray estimates that 20,000 people were shot, "of whom three-fourths had not taken part in the fight". The government's *official* total of summary executions was 17,000. Other estimates are up to 35,000.[220] Tens of thousands more fled, where imprisoned or deported.

To survive the Commune would have needed the revolution to spread far beyond Paris, linking up with smaller towns and rural communities. It would also have needed a more organised military defence and the Commune's leadership certainly failed in places to prepare for the inevitable attack. In particular, a march on Versailles before Thiers could have consolidated his forces would have bought much needed time for the Commune to establish itself and spread its revolutionary message. The drowning of the Paris Commune in blood did not prevent its lessons and legacy educating and inspiring workers around the world. Writing for the 40th anniversary of the Commune, Lenin said that the "cause of the Commune is the social revolution, the cause of the complete political and economic emancipation of the toilers. It is the cause of the proletariat of the whole world. And in this sense it is immortal".[221]

Russian Revolution 1917

The Russian Revolution of 1917 was the most momentous event in working class history.[223] When workers, peasants and soldiers seized power in Russia in October of that year it changed the world. The ordinary people of Russia showed that it was possible to overthrow oppressive, exploitative rulers and create a society run by workers and peasants.[224] In doing so, they helped put an end to the First World War, up until that point the most horrific conflict ever fought. They gave inspiration to oppressed peoples' everywhere and sparked revolution across Europe. While belligerent nation-states were fighting each other in the trenches of the First World War, Russian workers raised the banner of internationalism—showing that working people had to unite against the capitalists and generals who would set them against each other.

The revolution was a mass uprising of workers and peasants who overthrow the Russian monarch, the Tsar, and then went on to overthrow the new capitalist order. Key to the success of the revolution was the Bolshevik Party, a mass organisation of revolutionary workers, led by Vladimir Lenin. Lenin was born in 1870, and had spent much of his life organising the Russian Revolutionary workers movement. He was an important Marxist thinker, and one of the most important revolutionary theorists.

Over a century later, 1917 and what happened afterward, remains a touchstone for socialists, but at the time it was a lightning rod to the workers movement around the globe. It inspired revolutionary movements in Europe, particularly in Germany, where at the end of 1918, workers, sailors and soldiers stopped work, mutinied and set up workers' councils in emulation of their sisters and brothers in Russia. For a few months, it looked like revolution would spread from Russia across Europe, bringing down the capitalist nations whose conflict had led to millions of lives being lost.

The war was the context for the Russian Revolution. For years preceding the outbreak of the First World War, the socialist left had warned, and organised, against imperialist conflict. Socialists across the world had pledged that when war began, they would organise to stop the conflict. Resolutions at countless meetings and demonstrations committed the workers' movement to peace. Yet, in August 1914, when war did start the vast majority of the socialist movement capitulated and supported their own capitalist ruling class. Nowhere was this more shocking than in Germany where socialists were organised in the Social Democratic Party (SPD).

With a few exceptions, the international left capitulated to supporting its own nation-states. In Russia, the Bolsheviks' opposed the war and in Germany, a few revolutionaries around Rosa Luxemburg and Karl Liebknecht did the same. In almost every other country revolutionary opposition to the war was limited to a handful of socialists. Lenin worked tirelessly to argue against the imperialist war that it was the duty of socialists to call for the defeat of their own ruling class. Initially anti-war voices struggled to be heard. The outbreak of war silenced and marginalised socialist voices in every country, as the capitalists used the conflict to argue for national unity against opposing countries. Nevertheless the reality of war—enormous death in the trenches and shortages at home—began to push people to question and resist the war.

Russia in 1917 was a backward economy dominated by the peasantry. But the previous decade had seen the growth of capitalist industry in major cities like Petrograd and Moscow. This also meant the development of a powerful working class. When the war broke out, socialist organisation in Russia was underground, but as the war continued revolutionaries began to get a hearing. Lenin's Bolshevik Party had fought a long and difficult struggle to build the Russian socialist movement. As the war progressed, they increased their agitation, gaining confidence as anger at the war increased.

Growing discontent affected places even where pro war feeling had been intense. In his history of a Moscow metal factory during the Russian Revolution, Kevin Murphy tells how the workers there went from organising anti-German pogroms in May 1915, to protests and strikes over conditions and pay a few weeks later. They were encouraged in this by Bolshevik activists in the factory.

One recalled, "comrades again renewed work that had

been interrupted", and another worker recounted "Our skilled workers began discussion about political events... that the Tsar was a fool incapable of governing and that Rasputin ruled Russia." The Bolsheviks' even put up leaflets in the toilets calling for "the overthrow of the Tsar, for arming workers". By August 1915 a strike by 650 workers in the factory won a "small wage increase". Despite repression, there were growing economic and political strikes through to 1917, strikes that began to take up wider issues. A May 1916 strike in the factory called for, "doubling sick pay; minimum wages of 15 kopecks for apprentices and women, 25 kopecks for male workers, and 30 kopecks for skilled workers; ending work at 2:30 on Saturdays and the day before holidays; and issuing wages and bonus pay on Saturday".[225]

Factories and workplaces around the country were going through exactly the same process of radicalisation. The experience in Moscow reflected the "class polarisation evident throughout Russian society".[226]

In early 1917, growing discontent at war, poverty and conditions in Russia exploded in revolution. It began in the capital Petrograd on 23 February 1917, as women sick of high prices, low wages and food shortages organised a protest for International Women's Day. They demanded male workers join them, marching and chanting "Down with the War! Down with high prices. Down with hunger!

One eyewitness recalled, "The women, driven to desperation by starvation and war, came along like a hurricane that destroys everything in its path with the violence of an elemental force. This revolutionary march of working women, full of hatred of centuries of oppression, was the spark that set light to the flame of the February revolution".[227]

The protests and strikes grew, within a day a general strike was spreading across the cities and despite some troops firing on workers' demonstrations, key regiments refused to shoot. Within days of the initial protests, the whole of Petrograd was shut down and the army in open mutiny. 27 February saw the foundation of the Petrograd Soviet of Workers' Deputies. This body, of elected delegates from different factories throughout the city, had existed during Russia's "dress rehearsal" revolution of 1905. Quickly the Soviet organised to arrest the Tsar's ministers and on the 2 March the Tsar abdicated. In barely a week, a mass revolution of working women and men had toppled a monarchy that had ruled for centuries. In the major cities of Russia, workers had begun to take control of their workplaces, kicking out the bosses and electing councils to manage the factories and organise the workers' movement. It was the beginning of a revolutionary process when workers' power would challenge the new capitalist government.

The fall of the Tsar did not mean the end of the revolution—it put power in the hands of a new ruling class, the capitalists. They celebrated the fall of the Tsar, but wanted the revolution to end there, so they could build up capitalism in Russia. Tsarism had been a barrier to the development of capitalism. For the capitalists the fall of the Tsar was the opportunity to build a modern Russian state—a capitalist society. It also meant continuing the war against Germany, to protect Russia's interests and its empire. For this to happen the rebellious workers and peasants had to stop their demands and end their revolution. There was no room for workers' power. This caused a contradiction. The war was creating a social and political crisis for the majority of the population, and the toppling of the Tsar could not solve this crisis. People were hungry, sick of the war and facing enormous poverty.

The revolutionary movement that had overthrown the Tsar gave worker's confidence to continue fighting and demanding more. The February Revolution saw workers in factories and workplaces throughout the country creating workers councils and soviets. These bodies were simultaneously organisations where workers and soldiers could come together to discuss action and organise their workplaces. They allowed coordination between groups of workers in different workplaces and across cities. By October, historian S A Smith says, "There were no fewer than ninety-four unified centres of factory committees (in towns, provinces, or branches of industry), together with an All-Russian Central Council of Factory Committees, committed to establishing workers' control of production across the entire economy".[228]

After the February Revolution a situation of "dual power" arose in Russia. On the one hand there was the new capitalist provisional government and on the other, the workers' institutions. The Bolshevik leader Lenin explained:

> This dual power is evident in the existence of two governments: one is the main, the real, the actual government of the bourgeoisie, the "Provisional Government"... which holds in its hands all the organs of power; the other is a supplementary and parallel government, a "controlling" government in the shape of the Petrograd Soviet of Workers' and Soldiers' Deputies, which holds no organs of state power, but directly rests on the support of an obvious and indisputable majority of the people, on the armed workers and soldiers.[229]

Lenin continued by pointing out that the overthrow of the Tsar had placed power in the hands of the bourgeoisie—the capitalist class—while simultaneously moving towards a "revolutionary-democratic dictatorship of the proletariat and the peasantry" based on the power of the soviets and resting on the force of the masses.

Such a situation was unstable. Ultimately, only one power could exist. The contradiction of dual power would be resolved either with the workers overthrowing the Provisional Government or through defeat of the soviets by the capitalists.

As 1917 continued, the crisis grew worse. Production of essentials collapsed and factories and workplaces had to close. Millions of workers lost their jobs, food and fuel was in short supply and the value of wages fell. The Bolsheviks raised the slogan of "Bread, Peace and Land", uniting the demands of the workers' and the peasantry. The context of dual power meant that the possibility of workers' power was constantly raised as a potential resolution to the crisis. As S A Smith explains,

> Between February and October [1917] 2.5 million workers downed tools and the average strike increased in size as the year wore on. Yet strikes also became harder to win, especially on wage issues. As they became less effective, the trade unions made efforts to negotiate collective wage agreements for entire industries. But negotiations proved intractable and no sooner had new contracts been ratified than they were nullified by inflation. The other response to the economic crisis, pursued by the factory committees, was to implement workers' control of production to prevent what workers believed was widespread 'sabotage' being practised by employers.[230]

Workers' control was a "practical response" to the growing economic and political crisis. The bodies that could organise this, the soviets and workers' councils were the basis for a society based on workers' power. Today popular accounts of the Russian Revolution often downplay or ignore the role of the soviets. Yet understanding how these bodies work is key to understanding how workers' can run society. Contemporary accounts of soviets in the Russian Revolution demonstrate the link between mass democracy and workers' power.

The American socialist and journalist John Reed wrote this description based on his experiences in Russia in 1917:

> There is today in Moscow and throughout all the towns and cities of Russia a complex political structure upheld by the vast majority of the people and which is functioning as well as any new-born popular government ever functioned.
>
> The soviet is based directly upon the workers in the factories and the peasants in the fields; the Petrograd Soviet of Workers' and Soldiers' Deputies serves as an

> example. It consisted of about 1,200 elected deputies and held plenary sessions every two weeks.
>
> It elected a central executive committee of 110 members based on party proportionality and this central executive committee invited delegates from all the political parties, from the union committees, the factory shop committees and other democratic organisations... there were also ward soviets made up of the deputies elected from each ward... In some parts of the city there were no factories and therefore normally no representation of those wards... But the soviet system is extremely flexible, and if the cooks and waiters, or the street sweepers or the courtyard servants or the taxi drivers of that ward demanded representation they were allowed delegates.
>
> Elections of delegates are based on proportional representation, which means the political parties are represented in proportion to the number of voters in the whole of the city. And it is political parties and programmes that are voted for, not candidates... The delegates are not elected for any particular term, but are subject to recall at any time. No political body more sensitive and responsive to the political will was ever invented.[231]

Permanent Revolution

Before 1917 most Russian Marxists thought that the coming revolution would be a bourgeois one, analogous to the revolutions that had overthrown the feudal monarchies of France and England. They believed that the revolution would introduce a capitalist society that would develop the Russian economy to the point when a socialist revolution would be possible.

The revolutionary Leon Trotsky held a different view. He had led the Petrograd Soviet in the 1905 Revolution, and the experience of this workers' struggle led him to realise that the political revolution against the Tsar over democratic demands would "grow over" into a wider revolution over economic demands. The advanced development of industry within Tsarist Russia meant that workers did not have to wait for the further development of capitalism before fighting for socialism. Trotsky called this theory "Permanent Revolution" and developed it from the experience of 1905 and the ideas of Marx and Engels.

Marx and Engels had written extensively on bourgeois revolutions. They based much of their understanding of these on the experience of the French Revolution of 1789. In 1789 the French bourgeoisie was a revolutionary class, overthrowing (and executing the monarch) and developing bourgeois society. Most revolutionaries, including Marx and Engels, thought that similar processes would take place in other countries—overthrowing feudal aristocracies and creating bourgeois capitalist societies. Marx and Engels' experience of the development of the bourgeoisie in Germany in the 1830s and 1840s, led them to break from this view. They increasingly saw the German bourgeoisie as unwilling to carry through a revolution against feudalism because of its fear of the growing power of the working class.

Marx argued that the emerging German working class would be the power that would drive through a revolution against feudalism, but then go much further.[232] Following the defeat of the bourgeois revolutions in Germany in 1848, Marx concluded, "purely bourgeois revolution… is impossible… What is possible is either the feudal and absolutist counter-revolution or the social republican revolution".[233]

This approach informed Trotsky's theory of Permanent Revolution; he saw that the working class in Russia, despite its relatively small size, could overthrow the Tsar's regime, but could also continue on to lead a fight for a socialist society. When Lenin arrived in Russia in 1917 he immediately began, to the shock of many of his comrades in the Bolshevik Party, agitating for a further development of the revolution. Rather than fighting to consolidate a bourgeois state, the revolutionary workers had to continue to drive forward further revolutionary change, going beyond the overthrow of the Tsarist regime.

But in the context of Russia in 1917 there was a crucial final factor. Both Lenin and Trotsky believed that while workers' in Russia could overthrow the Tsar and move to a revolution against capitalism, they also knew that on its own the Russian Revolution would be isolated and defeated unless it spread to the more developed capitalist countries, principally those of Western Europe.

Internationalism

The nature of capitalism in the early 20th century, the reality of imperialist war, and the integration of Russia into a wider capitalist economy meant that the Russian Revolution made real the question of workers' emancipation through socialist revolution. Despite the growth of Russia's working class, and the huge, advanced, factories in places like Petrograd and Moscow, the country was still economically backward. For this reasons leading figures of the revolution like Lenin and Trotsky understood that unless the revolution spread to other countries, its isolation would lead to its defeat.

The dominance of peasant agriculture meant that a successful revolution would mean the working class leading the majority of the population—the peasantry—in a seizure of power. In 1917 the Russian peasantry shared many demands of the workers in the cities and towns, indeed the very fact that the Russian economy was only recently industrialised meant that there remained very close links between town and country.

The Russian army was predominantly peasant-based, and the war was hitting rural communities badly. Lenin and the Bolsheviks sought to develop the programme of the soviets to pull the peasantry closer to the revolutionary working class. Through 1917, the reality of war and crisis brought the workers movement closer and closer to the Bolsheviks. As Trotsky explained:

> The growth of strikes, and of the class struggle in general, almost automatically raised the influence of the Bolsheviks. In all cases where it was a question of life-interests the workers became convinced that the

> Bolsheviks had no ulterior motives, that they were concealing nothing, and that you could rely on them. In the hours of conflict all the workers tended toward the Bolsheviks, the non-party workers, the Social Revolutionaries, the Mensheviks. This is explained by the fact that the factory and shop committees, waging a struggle for the life of their factories against the sabotage of the administration and the proprietors, went over to the Bolsheviks much sooner than the Soviet. At a conference of the factory and shop committees of Petrograd and its environs at the beginning of June, the Bolshevik resolution won 335 out of 421 votes. This fact went by utterly unnoticed in the big newspapers. Nevertheless it meant that in the fundamental questions of economic life the Petrograd proletariat, not yet having broken with the Compromisers, had nevertheless as a fact gone over to the Bolsheviks.[234]

The role of the Bolshevik Party in 1917 proved decisive. The Mensheviks and the capitalists worked hard to undermine and hold back the development of workers' power. They were almost successful in this, and Lenin's party had to navigate complicated political terrain. However the Bolsheviks' focus on developing workers' power and the possibility of socialist revolution saw them win a majority in the soviets. Under Bolshevik influence, the workers' soviets led the seizure of power in October 1917.

When workers' took power in Russia, it gave inspiration to workers around the world. There was already growing discontent across Europe, and in November 1918 revolution swept Germany. Workers', soldiers' and sailors' councils appeared across the country, but unlike in Russia, there was no equivalent of the Bolshevik Party to argue for workers' power. The lack of revolutionary leadership meant that Social Democrats were able to use the revolutionary movement to place themselves at the head of a parliamentary government—undermining the revolutionary dynamic. At the same time, counter-revolutionary forces, including forerunners of fascist groups, destroyed the revolutionary left. Short-lived workers' councils also appeared in countries like Ireland and Hungary. Even in Britain, 1919 saw a wave of mass strikes that reached nearly insurrectionary proportions. The failure of these movements to take power left Russia isolated.

Nonetheless, the Russian Revolution transformed ordinary people's lives in the years immediately after the seizure of power. The Soviets nationalised the land and local communities were put in charge of redistributing land that formerly belonged to rich landlords, the church and the crown to the peasantry. Before the revolution, Russia had been a highly oppressive, religious, society. Women were liberated by the revolution—the church no longer oversaw marriage, which became a voluntary relationship. Divorce was made straightforward, abortion legalised and homosexuality decriminalised. The new government recognised the rights of national minorities and gave oppressed countries the right to self-determination.

The Soviet government systematically challenged antisemitism, and began mass campaigns to improve literacy and education. Revolutionary Russia saw an explosion of interest in arts and culture, with debating halls, lecture theatres, concerts and operas filled to capacity.

But the new revolutionary society would not be built by decrees from above, but instead by action from below. At a meeting of the All-Russia Central Executive Committee immediately after the soviets took power, Lenin said:

> The local soviets, depending on time and place, can amend, enlarge and add to the basic provisions worked out by the government. Creative activity at the grass roots is the basic factor of the new public life. Let the workers set up workers' control at their factories. Let them supply the villages with manufactures in exchange for grain... Socialism cannot be decreed from above. Its spirit rejects the mechanical bureaucratic approach;

> living, creative socialism is the product of the masses themselves.[235]

Counter-revolution

Almost as soon as the soviets took power in 1917, the capitalists tried to undermine and defeat the revolution.[236] The victory of the revolution took Russia out of the war. But, from 1918 a civil war was fought in Russia against Soviet power. Imperialist countries such as the US, France, Britain and Japan sent military forces into Russia to destroy the revolution.

The Russian working class, exhausted by years of war, responded magnificently to this challenge. Trotsky formed the Red Army, which defeated the counter-revolutionary armies but at enormous cost. Russia's workers, peasants and economy were exhausted. In cities like Petrograd and Moscow the best workers had joined the Red Army, including many of the Bolsheviks.

Conditions were appalling. Murphy explains that the end of the civil war "encouraged rising expectations among workers" and the end of 1920 and early 1921 saw a major strike wave across Russia. Strikes like these often were successful, but they demonstrated that the isolation of the Soviet Union internationally was badly damaging its position. One leading Bolshevik Alexander Shilapnikov said at the Bolshevik Congress in 1922, "Lenin said yesterday that the proletariat as a class, in the Marxist sense, does not exist. Permit me to congratulate you on being the vanguard of a non-existing class".[237]

The hollowing out of the Russian economy through civil war and economic isolation meant that the government had to introduce emergency plans. In 1921 the Bolsheviks' introduced the New Economic Policy (NEP) to try and encourage industrial development—it allowed private production and free markets to stimulate production, particularly in rural areas. Kevin Murphy traces the "ascendancy of the Stalinist system" from the introduction of the NEP. By 1928, the regime was confident enough to begin attacking workers' pay and conditions to fund the rapid industrial development of the First Five-Year Plan.[238]

Tomáš Tengely-Evans explains that a bureaucracy evolved which developed its own collective interests separate to those of the working class:

> The Soviet bureaucracy, in its attempts to hold society together in the 1920s, had to mediate between different social classes—namely workers and peasants. This meant keeping hold of the collectivist aims of the socialist revolution and appeasing the individualistic aspirations of the peasantry. While one can't doubt the Bolsheviks' socialist intentions in the 1920s, their own structures came to reflect the often antagonistic class forces it mediated between. The working class, which could have brought socialist pressure to bear, was alas the weakest and most disorganised one.[239]

By the end of the 1920s, the bureaucracy had developed into a ruling class with its own set of interests. The process was not automatic. Indeed Russia saw vigorous and intensive debates between different factions in the Soviet leadership about the direction of the economy. Joseph Stalin and those grouped around him, manoeuvred to defeat their opponents. Stalin and his supporters were the political representation of the Soviet bureaucracy's collective interests. Stalin consolidated his power with the systematic destruction of any opposition to him, including most of the "Old Bolsheviks" who had been the backbone of the revolutionary movement. Russia was no longer a socialist society created out of revolution. Democracy, previously so central to the revolutionary process, was curtailed. Workers' no longer had any control over production, industry being organised on a top down basis by the centralised bureaucracy. Repression and exploitation became the reality of working class life. After 1928, Russia was a state capitalist society whose interests and economic behaviour was driven by its ongoing competition with the rest of the capitalist world. The bureaucracy was forced to accumulate wealth to stay ahead of the Western powers. The development of capitalism in countries like Britain had seen a process of "primitive accumulation" driving the peasantry from the land and enclosing common land in order to form the basis for a new system of wage labour. In Stalinist Russia, the same process took place over a much shorter period, the peasantry was expropriated, forcibly collectivised, leading to massive famines that killed millions. Rather than the economy being geared towards satisfying the needs of Russia people, it was now organised for accumulation in competition with the west. While the collapse in living standards hit ordinary people hard, the state capitalist bureaucracy lived a privileged lifestyle, just like the ruling class of the capitalist states.[240]

Looking back on 1917, we should not judge the Russian Revolution by what the Soviet Union became. It should be celebrated as the most thoroughgoing attempt yet in history to transform society in the interests of the "associated producers", those whose labour makes society function. The institutions created by the workers, soldiers and peasants in the midst of the revolution showed the potential for the organisation of society in an entirely new way. The revolution challenged oppression, and showed how a socialist society might finally eradicate sexism, racism and homophobia.

The crucial lesson from Russia though is how the Bolsheviks' took the revolution forward, navigating the movement through the twists and turns of 1917 towards the victorious insurrection in October, which remains a model for revolutionaries today. Without that mass revolutionary party the workers' would not have taken power, and the movement would likely have been crushed by right-wing military forces during 1917. The Russian Revolution itself remains a beacon to show that workers' can organise to overthrow capitalism, and as such, its lessons for socialists today are myriad.

An ecological note to the Russian Revolution

In the 1900s the Moscow zoologist Grigorii Aleksandrovich Kozhevnikov was becoming increasingly concerned about the way that industrial development was destroying nature, particularly the destruction of biodiversity. He believed that the "encroachment of civilisation" was driving the extinction of species and argued for the conscious protection of "virgin nature" or it would "disappear entirely, and the nature transformed by civilisation which will replace it will only deceive us by its one-sided luxuriance, shadowing the image of the vanished past".[241]

In order to protect nature, Kozhevnikov argued for the creation of zapovedniki, special "nature reserves", where there was to be no hunting, no tourism, harvesting or agriculture. Nature would be left alone in these areas so "we may observe the result". [242] Kozhevnikov's ideas were widely taken up in the Russian and international scientific community and the first zapovedniki were created by the early 1900s in "diverse geographical settings". Despite such success, the Tsarist state "failed to fulfil even a fraction of the hopes that the conservationists had placed on it" as such, "in March 1917 few conservationists regretted the passing of the old regime."

Even in the midst of the revolution, activists and scientists were concerned about protecting and extending the zapovedniki. The Kronstadt Soviet of Soldiers' and Workers' Deputies, was so worried by the threat to the Askania-Nova zapovednik at the other end of the country, it passed a resolution calling on the government to send a commissar to protect it.[243] 1917 saw a renewed growth in conservation societies in Russia, and on the eve of the workers' seizure of power a large conservation conference met in Petrograd.

The chaos and destruction of the civil war period interrupted systematic work to protect ecology. But there were signs of the direction in which things might have gone. In May 1918 the Council of People's Commissars met and passed a motion "On Forests" intended to stop the unsustainable logging of forests. In April 1919 Lenin put his name to a "Decree for the Protection of Beekeeping" to protect beehives and apiarists. But the longest ecological legacy of this period was the new zapovedniki created after the revolution. Nikolai Nikolaevich Podvoisky came to

Moscow on a mission from Astrakhan where he was deputy commissar. One of the things he wanted to raise with the Soviet government was the creation of a zapovednik in the Volga. In 1919 he managed to get a meeting with Lenin. The Russian leader was enthusiastic, proposing that Podvoisky draw up a decree which was quickly authorised by Lenin.[244]

Tragically the civil war intervened, but in September 1921 a bill was passed entitled "on the Protection of Monuments of Nature, Gardens and Parks" authorising the creation of zapovedniki, protected along the lines of Kozhevnikov's suggestions. The areas protected in 1921 were the "first protected territory anywhere to be created by a government exclusively in the interest of the scientific study of nature".[245] Despite the restrictions posed by civil war, the fledgling Soviet government took matters of ecology seriously, basing its approach on the most radical scientific knowledge of the day. This contrasts with the approach of the later Stalinist regime, whose ecological understanding shows the same break with the revolutionary past as in other areas. This is best epitomised by the Stalinist official who called for a "profound rearrangement of the entire living world… all living nature will live, thrive and die at none other than the will of man and according to his plans".[246] Under state capitalism, just as under free market capitalism, the natural world became subordinated to the accumulation of capital.

Egyptian Revolution 2011

The revolutionary situation that developed in Egypt in 2011 saw millions of people overthrow a hated dictator. The revolution was the high point of a period of uprisings around the Middle East known as the Arab Spring. Mainstream accounts highlight the huge city square occupations that became emblematic of the uprising. Yet this overlooks the crucial involvement of millions of workers who shaped the revolution through their strikes and occupations. The Egyptian revolution demonstrated how revolutions transform consciousness. Individuals who felt powerless to protest or speak out found themselves organising and addressing huge demonstrations. Oppressed groups joined the demonstrations as people from different religions defended each other from repression. Crucially, Egypt in 2011 showed that workers' revolution is still on the agenda in the modern world and Egyptian workers showed that socialist revolution remains possible.

Looking back at the Egyptian Revolution, we can see once again that revolution is a process. Just as in Russia in 1917, once the initial uprising had won key demands—specifically the fall of the dictator Mubarak—revolutionaries had to navigate a twisting road. This road saw different challenges, the threat of the army and the state, and the competing interests of different organisations in Egyptian society like the Muslim Brotherhood. Finally, the revolution had to defend itself from external physical attacks. Missing in Egypt was a mass revolutionary organisation that could play the role the Bolsheviks played in 1917—helping the working class movement navigate these processes. While revolutionary socialists in Egypt did try to shape events, they were not big enough to influence key outcomes.

In December 2010 protests began in Tunisia after Mohamed Bouazizi, a street vendor, self-immolated in protest at repeated harassment by local officials. The Tunisian demonstrations brought down the country's President Zine El Abidine Ben Ali in January 2011, ending his 23-year reign. Tunisia's uprising inspired rebellion across the Middle East and North Africa, which in turn inspired further global protests, including the anti-austerity Spanish indignados and Occupy movements. Rebellions and uprisings took place in Oman, Yemen, Jordan, Egypt, Syria, Morocco, Iraq and Kuwait. In addition to Ben Ali, three other autocratic rulers fell—Muammar Gaddafi in Libya, Hosni Mubarak in Egypt and Ali Abdullah Saleh in Yemen. Revolution went furthest in Egypt where the revolution drew on decades of discontent, workers' struggles that had grown in confidence through the 2000s and, crucially, huge political discontent over the US-led war in Iraq and the oppression of the Palestinians.

Egypt was a long-time key ally of the United States in the Middle East. Egypt's links to the US helped stabilise the region in the interests of Western imperialism and give Israel freedom to attack the Palestinian people.[247] Mubarak allied himself with the US during the First Gulf War and provided support for the US occupations of Afghanistan and Iraq. Egypt's support for the US and Israel provoked huge anger—with protests in solidarity with the Palestinian Intifada in 2000 and against the Afghanistan and Iraq wars in the 2000s. The 2003 global anti-war protests saw a sit-in in Tahrir Square, the main central square in Egypt's capital Cairo. These protests were "the first time that pictures of Mubarak were torn down and burnt, and people made a direct link between opposition to the US war and opposition to the Mubarak regime"; they were the "first of several small-scale dress rehearsals for 2011".[248]

Another factor driving discontent with Mubarak was his regimes' commitment to neo-liberal policies. "Neoliberalism came early to Egypt" with attacks on the public sector and privatisation beginning in the 1970s. In the 1990s, Mubarak accelerated neoliberalism and by the end of the 2000s, the number of Egyptians living on less than two dollars a day had doubled.[249]

Together with the political protests against war and in solidarity with Palestine, the 2000s saw a parallel growth in industrial protest over economic issues. In December 2006, a strike wave began in Mahalla, a town in northern Egypt with a large textile industry. Unlike previous strikes which usually lasted a day, this one went on for two weeks and saw strikes spread through 2007 and 2008, "concentrated in the civil and public sector" but encompassing some private sector workplaces and workers who "had no history of militant strikes, including doctors, nurses, teachers, tax collectors and many others".[250]

Anne Alexander and Mostafa Bassiouny argue that the "rediscovery of the strike" tactic in Mahalla was a step forward from the previous key tactic under Mubarak of the sit-in as it directly affected production, and hence profits.[251]

Police prevented a further planned strike in Mahalla in April 2008, which provoked big demonstrations and rioting against buildings linked to the regime. The "April 6 Youth Movement" named itself from these events, which had involved tens of thousands in the city. This was, as Egyptian revolutionary Sameh Naguib says, the "second and more menacing dress rehearsal for the 2011 revolution".[252]

Finally, despite the repression and difficulties in organising, there was a growing movement for democracy, a "very broad alliance of opposition forces" called Kefaya, including "Nasserists, liberals, and several left-wing organisations, including the Egyptian Communist Party, the Revolutionary Socialists, and others" together with independent figures.

The demonstrations were relatively small, involving hundreds or perhaps a few thousand, but it encouraged larger forces, including the Muslim Brotherhood to "move in the same direction".[253]

Jack Shenker, the *Guardian's* former Egypt correspondent, explains the importance of these democracy movements:

> Kefaya as an organised force was not long-lasting... But the movement had served a crucial purpose, not least by normalising the sight of opposition protest on Egypt's streets and visibly challenging the regime's grip over public spaces.[254]

Shenker also points out that the use of highly militarised forces against protests undermined the "equation of Mubarak with stability and Egyptians with political inertia".[255]

By the time the Tunisian protests exploded Egypt had a working class movement that had grown in confidence and a small history of political protest over imperialism and democracy. It also had a regime that was not afraid of using violence to repress protests. As Egyptian socialist Hossam el-Hamalawy said, "On the eve of January 2011, Egypt was a classic case of what Russian revolutionary Vladimir Lenin described as a 'revolutionary situation'".[256]

The Egyptian Revolution began on 25 January 2011. Its context was the Tunisian uprising and the fall of Ben Ali, its background was decades of neoliberalism, war and oppression. Immediate motives included the rigged elections of November 2010, the state murder of blogger Khaled Said and the bombing of a Christian Coptic Church, which led to protests by Copts in Cairo. 25 January was to be a day of protest for democracy and against police violence, organisers expected a few thousand, but hundreds of thousands turned up.

Naguib explains what happened:

> As the numbers swelled the chants began to unify around what was by then the famous slogan of the Tunisian revolution: 'The people want to overthrow the regime'. The activists who had started the demonstrations had rapidly become a tiny minority. The attempts by police and riot forces to stop the growing movement using tear gas, rubber bullets and then live ammunition failed dramatically as the sheer numbers of the demonstrators completely overwhelmed the police forcing them to retreat... Now the thousands of soldiers were surrounded by far larger numbers... eventually leading to the disintegration of the whole police force. The leadership of the Muslim Brotherhood, the largest opposition force in the country, issued statements against participation in the January 25th demonstrations. This did not stop thousands of their youth taking part on the day.[257]

Police stations across Egypt were burnt as protesters defied curfews and violence to stay on the streets. Tahrir Square became the emblematic centrepiece of the revolution, where thousands of protesters gathered to organise, debate and plan. Food, water, toilets and medical aid were provided and the movement organised to protect itself.

British socialist Judith Orr headed to Cairo to report on the revolution for *Socialist Worker*. These extracts from her online diary give a sense of the mood in Tahrir:

> Sun 30 Jan, noon
> Many people have spent the night in the square, only taking a break for a smoke and a tea in the After Eight cafe which stayed open all night. They lie exhausted on the grass in the centre of the square. Some have bloody bandages round their heads. But fresh waves of protesters keep coming to join them. They arrive from all corners of Cairo and swarm past the soldiers and their desert camouflaged tanks. The protesters greet the soldiers as old friends. They hug and kiss and give each other high fives. They clamber up on the tanks to chant and hold up home-made placards. One tank has "Fuck Mubarak" spayed on its side.
>
> Sun 30 Jan, 8pm
> I walk down one of the major avenues off Tahrir Square. Every road running off the square has a barricade and a committee checking cars. Some people have set up chairs and a fire outside their shoe shop. Two men sitting on plastic deck chairs stop me to welcome me to Egypt. They say that [they] will be there all night to protect the offices they work in. "We are here until it's finished", they say. People agree that there was widespread looting on Friday, but everyone blames the police. They describe the police going on a rampage. It seems that the police wanted to create fear and chaos so that people would miss Mubarak's strong hand. It hasn't worked. People have taken their lives into their own hands. At the edge of the square, the number of tanks has grown to nine. But still they are surrounded by chanting protesters who barely stop to take a breath. Elsewhere people are bedding down in doorways for the night.

Sun 30 Jan, midnight
Police have been seen in some parts of the city but not in Tahrir Square. "They wouldn't dare show their faces here" said one young guy on checkpoint duty on a barricade. They wear white makeshift sashes and are keeping the streets clean as well as providing security. A woman comes up and asks if the way to her home is safe. Two men are dispatched to make sure she can get through.

Sun 30 Jan, 1am
The medical care in Tahrir Square is well organised. but they have run out of basic medicines. At night, doctors sleep in a designated area so people know where to get help. Major injuries are taken to the temporary hospital in a nearby mosque. Around all the homes in the area collections for money and goods are done. One doctor said "What more can we do. We can look after ourselves but we need to be able to care for the sick and wounded. I want everyone to know what we are up against".

Mon 31 Jan, 5.30pm
What is amazing about watching events like these is the speed of change in people. Almost no one I speak to has been a political activist before now. It wasn't easy for anyone to be politically active under this regime but what has happened this week is that a deep bed of bitterness has been exposed. People who had struggled to survive and felt powerless to challenge the way they were treated now feel that they are in charge. They are indignant that Mubarak is still clinging on but are entirely confident that they will win. And every hour the Tahrir Square is getting fuller. This is the biggest day so far. Some say 300,000 are on the streets right now—it certainly looks like it.[258]

The scale of the sit-in in Tahrir Square was symbolic of the revolution itself. But Shenker cautions us that...

> ...there is a danger in projecting too much of the revolution on to this single square, and thus confining the revolution in space and time... Focusing too closely on Tahrir ignores a panoply of revolutionary struggles, and it leaves the factories and farms and schools and alleyways and minds in which revolution is raging dangling far off the edge of the page, alongside the dozens of other city squares across Egypt where battles were won and occupations mounted.

Nonetheless he continues:

> Tahrir was special. Not because it was all the revolution consisted of... because it embodied something more fundamental about the revolution—an action of creation, one that has coloured Egypt's politics irrevocably ever since. In Tahrir, Egyptians built something different from Mubarak Country: a different set of borders, a different set of social relations, a different narrative about who they were and what they could do. [259]

Millions of people were taking part in the revolution. As even bigger protests took place on 1 February, an Egyptian army spokesperson announced that soldiers would not shoot protesters. The generals were fearful that a violent crackdown would split the army and turn thousands of rank-and-file socialists against them. [260] The day before the protests, the government announced it would begin discussions with opposition groups.

Two million demonstrated in Tahrir Square, 1 million in Alexandria, 750,000 in Mansoura and 250,000 in Suez. The protests forced Mubarak to address the country and promise not to seek re-election. The following day, thousands of violent thugs, organised by one of Mubarak's sons, attacked Tahrir.

The day saw pitched battles as revolutionaries defended their space against heavily armed thugs and police snipers. Thousands of people were injured and over a dozen killed, but by the morning of 3 February, the counter-revolutionary forces had been driven off.

This victory boosted the revolution and brought thousands back onto the streets in solidarity. That Friday was designated "departure day" with protesters calling demonstrations after Friday prayers to call on Mubarak to go. Millions of people joined these protests. In Tahrir Square the unity of revolution was on display as Coptic Christians, together with people of no faith formed lines to protect Muslims at prayer. The government had announced that on 6 February it would negotiate with opposition organisations. These included several tame and unthreatening groups, but crucially several key leaders of the Muslim Brotherhood. The response from the streets to these tame negotiations was anger. In particular, the young people of the Muslim Brotherhood who had played a central role in defending Tahrir squares against the government's thugs during the "battle of the camel" attacked their leaders for joining talks that they saw as selling out the revolution. Under pressure, the Muslim Brotherhood's leadership announced the talks had failed. [261]

The same day as these failed talks, the organised working class joined the revolution. This was a crucial development. 300,000 workers joined a wave of strikes over the following three days. Naguib argues that the strikes were important because they:

> ...carried the revolution into state institutions, paralysing them and therefore indirectly strengthening the revolution in the squares. The strike wave included public transport workers, government hospital workers, postal workers, sanitation workers and workers in state-owned enterprises including six thousand workers serving the Suez Canal. Second, many of the strikes targeted the

> corrupt functionaries of Mubarak's ruling party with demands that institutions be "cleansed" or purged of all corrupt officials. This played a further role in paralysing the once powerful networks and resources of the ruling NDP (National Democratic Party).[262]

The effect of workers withdrawing their labour, brought more onto the streets, shut down the economy and gave confidence to those occupying the streets. It was enough for the Egyptian ruling class who announced that Mubarak had stepped down. Millions of Egyptians partied into the night.

The euphoria masked a wider problem. Mubarak had gone, but the military state that had supported him through decades of rule remained. The generals had kicked out Mubarak because they needed to save themselves.[263]

The Supreme Council of the Armed Forces (SCAF) now began to rule. On 13 February, they dissolved parliament and suspended the constitution, but no move was made to get rid of Mubarak's government. Protests continued as Egyptians celebrated the defeat of Mubarak and demanded the end of his government. SCAF's strategy was twofold. They needed to end the protests and strikes and introduce change that would leave the "main levers of state power... firmly in the hands of the military". In particular, there was a systematic campaign by SCAF, the Muslim Brotherhood and other parties to end the strikes.[264]

Naguib argues that this alliance between the Muslim Brotherhood and SCAF, "did not succeed in ending the revolution" but it did "divide the opposition". Strikes in particular continued to spread. SCAF introduced a law on 23 March to criminalise strikes and protests "that disrupt the normal function of institutions or services". [265] These did not succeed in stopping protests, with huge demonstrations on 1 April calling for the "banning of the NDP and for speeding up the process of investigating corruption and putting Mubarak, his sons, and other top officials on trial". In response SCAF made more concessions, arresting key former officials.

The summer would see further deepening of the protests and strikes, and...

> ...oppressed sections of society began expressing their own demands and organising against discrimination and oppression. Women, the Coptic minority, the Nubian community in the South, and Egyptians of the Sinai Peninsula all came out to express their anger and their demands against a state that had systematically oppressed them... for generations.[266]

But April also saw the beginnings of SCAF's attempts to restrict protests. Officers who joined demonstrations were arrested and military police fired on demonstrators. The forces of counter-revolution were mobilising and positioning themselves.

SCAF and the Muslim Brotherhood came together out of necessity, but the alliance was unstable. The Brotherhood wanted to ensure it had a role in the post-Mubarak regime, but its mass membership was central to the revolution on the streets and in the workplaces. In order to preserve their positions the leaders of the Brotherhood had to be seen to stand up to SCAF plans when they went too far. This happened in November when SCAF proposed constitutional changes to reduce parliamentary power and protect the role of the army. A mass protest occupation of Tahrir Square began again in response, with Muslim Brotherhood support, but now:

> There were deep division on the streets. The Islamists, despite their mobilisation, were limited to demanding the complete withdrawal of the constitutional proposals and to move on with the elections. The radical left and youth movements wanted to continue and deepen the mobilisation and turn it into a new wave of demonstrations and occupations until there were concrete concessions by SCAF.[267]

State violence saw many people killed and injured, but SCAF did announce some concessions. This was enough for the Muslim Brotherhood's leadership to pull out of the protests.

The next stages of the revolutionary movement saw growing divisions between different wings. The opening days of a revolutionary movement are always marked by excitement, unity and euphoria. Early victories inspire and bring more forces into the movement and there is a sense of unity and power. But as the revolution encounters opposition, challenges and counter-revolution, these raise questions of strategy and tactics. Unity is easy around single demands—the ousting of a dictator for instance—but as a revolutionary movement develops, the challenges posed pull the movement in different directions.

The summer and autumn of 2011 saw this process take place in Egypt, and in November when the first free and democratic elections took place, the movement was pulled in further directions. For some, particularly the Muslim Brotherhood and some left organisations, these elections were a victory. For others, particularly young people, the elections were a diversion. Many young people boycotted the elections.

The left and liberals did badly in the elections which ended in January 2012. The main victors were the Freedom and Justice Party, a coalition whose main constituent group was the Muslim Brotherhood, and the Islamic Alliance. Later presidential elections saw the Muslim Brotherhood's Mohamed Morsi only narrowly defeating Ahmed Shafiq, an "openly counterrevolutionary candidate". Shafiq's success reflected how the old state apparatus had rebuilt using "an openly counterrevolutionary 'law and order' campaign" attractive to the middle classes".[268]

In the second round, Morsi beat Shafiq, by 13.2 million to 12.3 million votes. While the election was a clear choice between revolution and counter-revolution, Morsi himself was no revolutionary. SCAF now manoeuvred to protect itself, using the Supreme Court to invalidate the parliamentary elections and changing the constitution to ensure that Morsi had few powers. Morsi proved unable to break free from the military, making concession after concession to SCAF. As Naguib explains:

> The Brotherhood's plan was to become accepted as a partner in power in return for containing the revolution and keeping intact the privileges and wealth of Mubarak's generals and businessmen and their regional and global allies. Instead of relying on mass mobilizations and a return to the squares to force concessions from Mubarak's men, they went in the opposite direction. Their rhetoric became that of law and order and the need for social peace.[269]

Opposition to Morsi took several forms. There were those that looked back to the "stability" of the Mubarak era, who saw the revolution as the problem. Then there were those that saw Morsi as the problem taking the revolution in the direction of an Islamic theocracy, and finally there was the opposition "based on the revolutionary movements that had opposed both Mubarak and the rule of the SCAF... This opposition wanted to develop the revolutionary process, both socially and politically, and saw Morsi and the Brotherhood as an obstacle".[270] New cycles of protest grew through 2012 into 2013 culminating in major mobilisations in June 2013. Despite the scale of these demonstrations, they were not a repeat of 2011. While they used the methods of the revolutionary movement, it was "mainly a counterrevolutionary mobilisation".[271] Counter-revolution, like revolution, can have a mass face, as the right mobilise the maximum forces in the street to challenge the power of the workers' movement. It is at moments like these when a mass revolutionary party becomes essential.

The July 2013 demonstration gave confidence to the military and on 3 July 2013 they launched a coup. Mass mobilisations by the Muslim Brotherhood brought thousands onto the streets, but General Abdel Fattah Al-Sisi, Morsi's minister of defence, ordered the army in. On 14 August 2013, at least 1,000 people were massacred. After defeating the Muslim Brotherhood, Al-Sisi turned on the left. Today about 60,000 activists are trapped in Egypt's prisons.

The military dominated the new regime even more, and "the neoliberal onslaught since the coup has been unprecedented." It is not a "restoration" of Mubarak era-government but a "qualitative shift to a new model of authoritarian neoliberalism… Capitalism with a monstrous military face".[272]

Was this inevitable? Writing ten years after the fall of Mubarak, el-Hamalawy argues that the revolutionary left was too small to shape events in the direction needed:

> A genuine mass revolutionary party, that could provide leadership for the strike wave [in February 2011], didn't exist. So the revolution was dominated by the reformist opposition. It pushed for a polarisation in the political scene along secular/Islamist lines, instead of polarisation over class.[273]

The outcome of revolutions is never automatic. The twists and turns that a revolution goes through arise out of concrete situations, and the response to this will depend on the balance of forces, the dominant ideas in the revolution and the political organisation. The objective causes of the revolution—poverty, unemployment and lack of democracy—remain. Al-Sisi's regime cannot solve those problems. In addition, Egypt is particularly vulnerable to the global situation. Egypt is the world's biggest importer of wheat. Russia and Ukraine are two of the world's biggest exporters, and Russia's invasion of Ukraine caused enormous financial problems for the Egyptian state as food prices spiked. Some 70 million Egyptians rely on a government-subsidised food programme, and in March 2022, the government went to the IMF for help.[274]

As the IMF representative for Egypt pointed out, "The rapidly changing global environment and spillovers related to the war in Ukraine are posing important challenges for countries around the world, including Egypt". War and global warming will only make the situation for Egypt's military rulers harder. There is certainly a fear in ruling circles that food shortages and increasing prices could provoke rebellion in the Middle East,

In March 2022, the *Financial Times* reported:

> Although grain prices have come down from the record highs hit immediately after the Russian attack, uncertainty surrounding exports from both countries have kept wheat prices two-thirds higher than a year ago. Sharp spikes in food prices are closely linked to social instability. A food crisis in 2007-08 caused by droughts in key wheat and rice-producing countries and a surge in energy prices led to riots in more than 40 countries around the world.[275]

It is impossible to predict whether a new Egyptian revolution might begin in the near future. We can say that the contradictions that led to the outbreak of the 2011 revolution remain, and in many ways, they have deepened. The only force capable of challenging those contradictions will be the Egyptian masses, who from 2011 to 2013 showed their bravery and capacity for organisation. New forces will need to rebuild the movement, its trade unions and crucially revolutionary socialist organisation. In doing so the experience of the Egyptian Revolution offers lessons and inspiration for the battles ahead.

Revolution in Sudan 2019-2022

On 11 April 2019, Sudan's President Omar al-Bashir was kicked out of office by the country's military forces. His 30 year rule was marked by war, mass murder, crimes against humanity and huge levels of poverty and inequality. Months of protests, sit-ins and workers' strikes drove him out in a mass revolution from below, a movement that also threatened wider sections of the Sudanese elite. Since then Sudan has experienced three years of a revolutionary process, involving millions of people struggling against a ruthless government prepared to use extensive violence against its opponents. Sudan shows that revolution is possible in the modern world, but it also teaches us that bravery and ingenuity from workers and the poor is not enough—we need revolutionary organisation and workers' power to overcome the state.

Viral posts from the protests and the key sit-in outside Bashir's military compound showed how the revolution was drawing strength from wide sections of the Sudanese population. Women were at the forefront of the revolution. Islamic military rule had restricted women, keeping them at home and making it impossible for them to have any public roles.[276] The revolution broke them free. Some of the most emblematic photos of the Sudanese revolution showed Alaa Salah speaking to a huge crowd from the roof of a car. Less well known was Aqadiyya Mahmoud Kuku, the head of the Tea Sellers' Union who played a central role in organising the sit-ins. In their history of the revolution up to spring 2022, authors Williow Berridge, Justin Lynch, Raga Makawi and Alex de Waal explain, "Women's activism [in the revolution] has subverted societal gender norms in new and provocative ways... Educated female protestors married and formed relationships with men encamped alongside them at army headquarters, often breaking convention by 'loudly proclaiming their desires' and choosing partners with little attention to their parents' class sensibilities".[277]

The revolution also rose to the challenge of racism. Delegations from Darfur joined the Khartoum sit-ins, despite the Bashir regime's use of racism against the Darfuris to divide and rule. "You arrogant racist, we are all Darfur!" chanted protesters against Bashir.[278]

The most visible aspect of the Sudanese revolution to the outside world was the sit-in outside military headquarters in Khartoum. At its height, this involved hundreds of thousands of people, inspired by but going beyond the similar mass protest in Tahrir Square during the Egyptian Revolution. David Pilling, writing in the *Financial Times* two weeks after the fall of Bashir wrote:

One cannot know for sure what Russia felt like in 1917 as the tsar was being toppled, or France in 1871 in the heady, idealistic days of the shortlived Paris Commune. But it must have felt something like Khartoum in April 2019.[279]

One eyewitness to the revolution, describes the sit-in:

As you walk into the area of the capital Khartoum now completely controlled by the young 'revolutionaries' down town, you see the difference. Street outside: full of rubbish with plastic bags strewn across the roads. Street inside: clean of rubbish—bags to put your garbage placed strategically around and young men with long hair and skinny jeans roaming around, picking up trash and encouraging others to help. People arranging prayer areas and ensuring privacy to do so. Volunteers organising checkpoints every few metres to ensure no one gets through with weapons. Women search women and men search men.

A pharmacy run by young volunteer pharmacists to dispense medication to those who need it. Medicine provided by companies and individuals for free. Two blood donation trucks to ensure those injured in the protests obtain the blood they need. People collecting cash contributions and bags of money left at the side of the road for anyone to take if they need money to get home. Shifts organised— the 'day revolutionaries' go home at night after the 'night revolutionaries' arrive to take over. Traditional Sudanese hospitality not forgotten—anyone visiting MUST drink tea or water. No cars allowed in unless you're bringing donations. No exceptions, even for foreign diplomats. The US ChargéD'Affaires was stopped outside when he came to visit. Street children being fed and looked after, included in this new society.

> Security? Taken care of. Makeshift blockades of bricks and borrowed razor wire block the roads to stop any attacks at night after a few failed but violent attempts to forcibly disperse the sit-in. Missing the football? Supporters sent a huge screen to watch the last big Barcelona match. Children are given flags and biscuits, carried on shoulders so they can see above the throngs of people. Birthday parties, weddings—you name it, it's happening right there in the street. Christian Sudanese Coptics holding fabric shades over the heads of their Muslim brothers while they pray under the hot sun. Without any 'leaders' whatsoever, these young Sudanese managed to effectively run this sit-in, this mini 'state' within the capital, and do so politely, without infighting, ego or provocation. Instead humour, cooperation, unity and solidarity are the order of the day.[280]

The sit-in, which arose out of a day of mass protests that converged on the centre of the capital, involved thousands of people from many different backgrounds debating, organising and living together in an ongoing protest. One participant described the "unintentional social melting", the coming together of many different sections of Sudanese society.[281] The sit-in, the growing protests on the streets as well as a limited number of strikes were enough to bring down Bashir, but it was not yet powerful enough to end military rule, a fact that the generals themselves understood.

In the aftermath of Bashir's defeat, one of the key revolutionary organisations, the Sudanese Professionals Association (SPA) issued a statement declaring the continuation of the movement:

> We assert that our revolution is continuing and will not

retreat or deviate from its path until we achieve our people's legitimate demands of handing over power to a civilian government.

The SPA continued:

We reaffirm once again that we will not retreat from the demands of the revolution. Our rallies in the national capital are in place and will not be disbanded and our civil disobedience continues until full arrival of our demands.

These were powerful and important words. But what was less clear was what the "demands of the revolution" were. Certainly, the SPA and the revolutionaries on the street wanted to see an end to military rule and a transition to democracy. However, the "leaders" of the revolution in the wider coalition that included the SPA, were unsure of how that transition would take place and what it would look like. In particular, how was the revolution going to oust the military leaders that had dominated Sudanese politics for decades?

In the aftermath of Bashir's fall, the opposition groups, organised together in the Forces of Freedom and Change (FFC), were unprepared for the new situation. They had come together around the clear demand of ending Bashir's rule but had no agreed plan for the next steps.

In contrast, the military generals who had put in place a transitional government understood that the longer they drew out negotiations, the more powerful their own position was. As Berridge and her co-authors explain:

Inside the negotiations with the FFC, the junta did not have to work hard to regain the upper hand. Whatever their internal frictions, the generals were astute enough to keep a common front when dealing with the civilians. They chipped away at civilian negotiators'

> credibility by pointing out basic errors they had made, like putting the wrong title of a law in a proposal. But such technical deficiencies were just glitches, albeit embarrassing ones. The core problem was the lack of internal structure or division of authority when it came to the FFC's efforts to bargain with the military. Different groups within the FCC had different goals and divergent tactics, and these came out into the open.

On the streets, the mood hardened. The fall of Bashir had led to a euphoric moment, but quickly as it became clear that the military were not going to give up power immediately the protesters returned to the streets. The day after Bashir's fall, Awad Ibn Auf, the general appointed to head the military council also resigned. As negotiations continued so did the protests on the streets. The negotiations stuck on the key issue of the balance of power between the military and civilians in the new government. On 28-29 May 2019, the opposition called a general strike. The SPA saw this as a peaceful mobilisation in order to achieve "full victory" against the military. The strike was hugely successful, and included "sugar workers at the Kenana and Sinnar factories, port workers, and general workers in the Kober industrial area in the capital Khartoum" and "health, petroleum, nuclear power, aviation, bank, telecom and civil service workers in several ministries, engineers and university lecturers".[282]

The strike demonstrated that Bashir's fall had not taken the wind from the revolution, but confusion within the FFC was weakening the movement. As the size of the main sit-in declined, the "FFC was slowly ripping apart; dissent came into the open. The gap between the street and the negotiators widened".[283] Crucially the FFC did not push for a solely civilian government.

On 3 June 2019, a few days after the general strike, the military made its move. The strike raised the stakes again, threatening the military and encouraging them to act against the revolution. The head of the military council lieutenant general Abdel Fattah al-Burhan sent in paramilitary forces against the sit-in, killing hundreds of protesters, committing mass rapes and destroying the encampment. The massacre was not just about smashing the physical representation of the revolution, but also destroying the core ideals, in particular the sexual violence against women protesters "looked like a deliberate targeting of the women, whose conspicuous role at the forefront of the protests had proved such a practical and symbolic challenge to the men in uniform".[284]

The violence against the revolution arose out of the military's recognition that the stalemate had to be broken, along with the threat posed by rising activity by workers, in particular the general strike. In this, the forces of the state showed a clearer understanding of the revolutionary moment than the negotiators. In response to the massacre, the SPA called workers onto the streets. This was the right tactic. The military was not going to compromise and if initiative was not to be lost, the revolution had to reassert its power.

A general strike on 11 June again brought millions of people onto the street, shutting down most of the Sudanese economy. This strike had the potential to force the military onto the back foot following the massacre, and begin to extend the revolution. But two days later the FFC leadership called the strike off and there was no alternative revolutionary socialist leadership to maintain it.[285]

This was an enormous mistake. As we have seen, earlier in the revolution, the mass street movement was enough to bring down Bashir. Up to mid-April, there had been few strikes though the SPA was wary of using this weapon. Writing before the 3 June massacre, Egyptian revolutionary el-Hamalawy warned of the threat to the revolution if workers' did not use their power:

> A general strike is necessary to confront the military council while preserving the peaceful character of the movement. In some places, and without waiting for the invitation of the SPA, workers and civil servants

> are mobilising in their factories and offices to demand permanent contracts, independent unions and to kick their managers from the old regime out of their workplaces. We saw this happen in Egypt in 2011, when Islamists and liberals went on the attack saying "strikes are selfish, now is not the time for them!"
>
> Yet these strikes are the beating heart of the revolution: escalating them into a general strike is a matter of life or death... Some may accuse the revolutionaries of trying to drag the country into a bloodbath. But the real bloodbath will be the inevitable blow by the generals against the revolution.[286]

In August 2019 the opposition signed an agreement with the Transitional Military Council, an interim government of six civilian and five military members, headed by lieutenant general al-Burhan with Abdalla Hamdok as Prime Minister. This was a "rotten" deal, which left the military in control giving it space to build its strength and undermine the revolution. [287]

Hamdok was not from the revolutionary movement, rather he was a former senior UN official; he promised reforms but was hamstrung by being in a coalition with the military. He was also a technocrat, committed to transforming the Sudanese economy through austerity. His minister of finance, Ibrahim Elbadawi was an economist from the World Bank and together they believed that solving Sudan's economic woes required austerity. In particular, this meant reducing subsidies on fuel and food, and devaluing the currency. "The subsidy is very high. It is close to 40 percent of our budget. It is a drain" said Hamdok. [288] For Sudan's poor such subsidies were essential.

The slow pace of change, the failure of the government to address the urgent needs of the Sudanese people and the continued presence of the military in the government led to a new phase of revolt in 2020, when mass protests of up to a million took to the streets again.

On 25 October 2021, General al-Burhan led the military in a coup. Civilian members of the Transitional Government were arrested and a state of emergency declared. The coup was the bitter outcome of the rotten deal signed in August 2019. The military had used the intervening months to strengthen its hand and try to undermine the revolution. The masses responded on an enormous scale in the following days. There were huge protests, including strikes and up to 2 million demonstrating across Sudan on the 30 October. Brutal repression by the military saw dozens of people killed and hundreds injured. Strikes and protests forced the military to restart joint rule in November and they reinstated Hamdok, but his position was now untenable. Demonstrations continued against military involvement in the government with protesters adding Hamdok's name "to the list of the disgraced". [289] In January 2022 he resigned.

It is not yet clear where the Sudanese revolution will head next. What is clear is that the revolutionary people have not yet been defeated, responding to each assault by the military with bravery. It is also clear that the military are also biding their time, trying to undermine the revolution by co-opting its leading figures and using state force to threaten and attack revolutionaries. The November 2021 coup is a warning that unless the revolution strengthens its position, using the power of the organised workers, the unstable compromise between civilian and military rule will not stand. The generals will likely try to reassert their rule. How to do this is the urgent task for the revolution, and its organisations such as the resistance committees.

For some, the Sudanese revolution has passed its peak. In their history of the revolution, Berridge and her colleagues describe the excitement and potential of the Khartoum sit-in that helped bring down Bashir in April 2019, but they draw pessimistic conclusions.

> This was a moment of Utopian revolution in Sudan, an inspiring promise that a different world was possible. For a few weeks, in one place, the fog of politics cleared

> enough for a remarkable congregation of Sudanese to create a space for a festival of a popular republic. It was euphoric: a generation's worth of ideals and aspirations released in an explosion of pride, protest and patriotism. It was a moment and a place where everything that divided Sudanese citizens was set aside, when citizenship and participation took on a heightened sense. Sudanese and non-Sudanese who joined the sit-in revelled in how the ordinary became extraordinary: the mazes of tea shops offering minty brew to resting revolutionaries; the chants and songs; the street art; the freedom of speech and association; and the sense of community. The sit-in coalesced around an egalitarian system of solidarity that stood in stark contradiction to the hierarchies and deal-making that still dominated the world outside its barricades. Anyone with human feelings was inspired. There was a democratic Sudan and it lasted 53 days—between the challenge to a dictator and a massacre.[290]

However, as I write this account, the revolution is not over. Understanding the potential for the Sudan revolution to win democracy and fight for a further transformation of society, requires looking beyond the superficial level of the sit-ins and asking where the alternative power to the generals lies. Crucially the working class needs to become the leading force in the Sudanese revolution through its own organisations. Tragically, the SPA saw the workers' movement as a stage army, to be called out when needed, rather than the potential basis for revolutionary power against the generals.

The failure to mobilise the strength of the working class led to two problems. Firstly, the lack of revolutionary working class organisations meant that no force was developed within the Sudanese revolution that could form an alternative leadership for the army rank and file. Recall the Russian Revolution. In 1917, the soviets of workers' and soldiers' deputies became an alternative power, organising both the revolution and beginning to take control of the economy through workers' councils. These organisations were able to win the loyalty of revolutionary soldiers, sick of war and the generals.

In the early stages of the Sudanese revolution, protesters began to win sections of the army to their cause. But without a permanent revolutionary pole of attraction that could break soldiers from the generals, this was slowly undermined. In revolutionary upheavals, workers' councils are the alternative power that shapes the revolution and shows the way forward to a different society.

Instances in revolution where the organisations of the revolution and those of the old state, vie for control of society are known as "dual power". Two sets of institutions, representing the old and new order, exist simultaneously. The actuality of workers' power pulls people towards it, breaking them from the old state. In particular, as in Russia in 1917, whole army regiments can come over to the councils, away from the influence of the senior officers and generals. Such a system is not stable in the long term—either the workers' movement will take power, or the old order will reassert control through counter-revolutionary means. In Sudan, the revolutionary forces were not powerful enough to break the mass of the army from its leaders.

The army used the period after Bashir's fall to consolidate their control over the state machine and the army. [291]

The revolution needed to break the power of its main enemy—the military—and the best way to do this was to continue to drive a wedge into the army, between the generals and the lower ranks. Had working class power grown it would have made this process much easier, building on the links between rank and file soldiers and the working class, and giving confidence to the rebellious soldiers. As el-Hamalawy wrote:

> The rebellion growing in the lower ranks of the officers and among soldiers was one of the main reasons for the junta's rush to get rid of Al Bashir, fearing the collapse

> of the army and the regime. These are the parts of the army that the revolutionaries should be seeking to negotiate and ally with, and whose participation they should be seeking.

Without workers' power developing in workplaces, there was no alternative base from which to extend the revolution. Strike committees and neighbourhood resistance committees had shown that the revolution was based on "self-organisation" from below. But on its own this was not yet an alternative source of power.

This is not to disparage the role of existing committees. In an important article about the revolution, Anne Alexander showed how resistance committees extended the revolution across the whole of Sudan.[292] In March and April 2021 there were over 5,000 resistance committees across Sudan. Alexander explains their functions:

> Resistance committees intervened to oversee the supply of flour to bakeries and the distribution of bread and cooking gas. At the beginning of the Covid-19 pandemic some sent out teams of activists to spread public health messages and distribute face masks and sanitiser.
>
> In many areas there is a formal division of labour between the neighbourhood political leadership in the Resistance Committee and a Change and Services Committee. This body brings together revolutionary activists working specifically on improving the delivery of services. Often this division of labour reflects a generational divide, with younger activists leading the resistance committee.
>
> Then there is the political education and movement-building work in the background. It draws in different generations of people to discuss and debate

slogans, tactics and strategy at local level.

In some cases, resistance committees have grown over from bootstrapped organisation for protests into democratic mass movement. They have elected general assemblies and executive committees, and delegates representing the neighbourhood on the local coordination.

These committees show that there is a basis for an alternative to military rule. Alexander reports that these committees were beginning to network, and in the aftermath of the October 2021 attempted coup they were starting to develop political programmes.

The huge street protests coupled with the intensifying cost-of-living crisis also re-opened the door to mass strikes, including by court workers, bank workers, health workers and teachers. However, the general strikes of May and June 2019 were not repeated. Alexander cautions that:

> The uneven growth of the revolutionary movement between the neighbourhoods and workplaces points to a difficult road ahead. Time will remain on the side of the generals and the ghouls unless new forms of revolutionary organisation emerge. Forms of revolutionary organisation which harness workers' strategic power to disrupt production, distribution and services and direct it at the repressive core of the state.

In an interview published in Spring 2022, Sudanese revolutionaries spoke of the development of the resistance committees:

> In recent weeks, we have seen the resistance committees drafting and putting out political declarations, which shows a certain maturation of the movement. Some

> of these declarations have been very interesting, and the way in which they are distributed and discussed is also encouraging. One that got significant attention was from the resistance committees in the city of Madani. In recent weeks, resistance committees in seven other Sudanese states have helped to redraft this declaration and have jointly adopted it as "The Revolutionary Charter for People's Power". The Madani resistance committees themselves sent it out for discussion by multiple means—emails, via Facebook and as voice notes on WhatsApp. They provided a WhatsApp number for people to get back in contact with suggestions and modifications. The Charter is more progressive than most other declarations, addressing economic issues directly. It thus represents a more leftist approach than many of the other resistance committees.[293]

They spoke of the mass participation, the democracy and the coordination of the resistance committees, which they said had "changed the way politics is done in Sudan".[294] But they warn that the working class has not yet developed the organisation capable of becoming the basis for an alternative power in Sudan, but that could change:

> In the short term [organised workers] can seriously harm al-Burhan's fragile military regime with strikes demanding improved wages and living conditions. Further struggles are expected due to the harsh austerity measures passed recently. In the long term, the workers' role will depend on the balance of forces between them and the ruling class. Committed revolutionaries will have to work among the working class, learning from them and providing them with the political education that will enable them to radically change society. The organised workers' movement will not go beyond economic demands spontaneously.[295]

The task for revolutionaries must be to develop a new form of economic power within Sudan that can challenge the military for power. This must be based on workers' councils. In particular, as Alexander highlights, there needs to be "coordination and solidarity within Sudan, across the divide between 'centre' and 'periphery' over the questions of peace and bread and land" which will help to break down differences between urban and rural areas.[296] It will point the way forward in the face of military repression. It can help build a "counter-power" to the military that can "make it possible to split the armed bodies of men at the core of the Sudanese state along class lines. This is what will turn the soldiers against their commanders".[297]

During the Russian Revolution, Lenin, following Trotsky's argument for "Permanent Revolution" argued that the Russian working class could make a revolution that would overthrow Tsarism, and then continue into a workers' revolution. Revolution in Russia, argued both Lenin and Trotsky, could not build socialism on its own, but could inspire international revolution—particularly in the developed economies of Europe. There are many parallels between this and the Sudanese situation. Sudan's economy is poor, yet its natural resources and its links to the wider international capitalist economy give its working class huge strategic power, and mean that a revolution against military rule raises far greater prospects for a transition to a new way of organising society than just a change from military rule to the neo-liberal democracy desired by Washington.

As I write this, it is not yet clear what the next stage of the revolution in Sudan will be. The experiences since the start of 2019 have created revolutionaries who can shape that process—arguing for a strategy that looks beyond simply overthrowing military rule and developing the organisation and combativeness of the Sudanese working class. Bringing those revolutionaries together in one organisation would enormously multiply their ability to influence events. As Muzan Alneel points out:

It will serve everyone much better if there was a clear revolutionary voice, supporting the revolutionary inclinations within existing resistance committees and providing sharp analysis. Without a revolutionary organisation we are at the mercy of individuals and social media algorithms.[298]

Chapter 8
The workers' state

In February 1917 the workers of Russia overthrew the Tsar. In making this revolution they created their own mass, democratic institutions, based on elected workplace councils and city wide soviets. The biggest, and most important, of these was the Petrograd Soviet, an organisation that brought together representatives from workplace councils and soldiers' regiments. As we have seen, the fall of the Tsar did not end the revolutionary crisis. The new government was pro-capitalist. While pleased to see the end of Tsarism, they wanted a new bourgeois state that would allow capitalism to flourish. In particular, the government wanted workers to return to work, peasants to stop rebelling and the war with Germany to continue. This would have meant an end to the revolution.

But the ordinary workers and peasants wanted peace as well as an end to the crushing economic crisis that was driving wages down and hunger and poverty up. This contradiction led to a continuation of the revolution as workers and peasants continued for fight for "Bread, Peace and Land". The result was a situation of dual power where two centres of power existed in society—the soviets, based on workers' power and the capitalist government. These two powers represented two conflicting interests in society—those of the exploiting class and the exploited. These interests cannot be resolved without one side defeating the other. A situation of dual power in a revolution can only be temporary.

After February 1917 the revolutionary situation in Russia was essentially about which side would win. The workers' and soldiers' councils and soviets in Russian society represented one power, but the capitalist state remained. States are not neutral—they are instruments of class rule, which in the last instance, retain the use of violence to suppress their class enemies. The capitalist state exists to protect the interests of the minority of the ruling class over the majority of the population who they exploit.

In Russia, the victory of the capitalist class would not have meant a peaceful end to the workers' and peasants' revolutionary movement. It would have seen mass repression, the destruction of institutions of workers' democracy and the suppression of revolutionaries as the capitalists reasserted their power and neutralised the workers' movement. This was not an abstract fear. The suppression of French revolutionary movement following the defeat of the Paris Commune had taken place within living memory. Russia had also had its own insight into counter-revolutionary danger when in August 1917, the far-right General Kornilov, had tried to march on Petrograd to destroy the revolution. The working population of Petrograd rose up to defend their city and their revolution, and Kornilov's forces melted away. The choice facing the people of Russia was not between bourgeois democracy and workers' power. The alternative to workers' power was a military dictatorship.[299] Finding a resolution for this was thus an urgent task for the revolution.

In the midst of the revolution, Lenin returned to the ideas of Marx and Engels to understand the problem of the state. He understood that at a certain point in a revolutionary process, the working class would have to supplant the capitalists and smash their existing state.

Lenin grappled with these ideas in several writings. In early October 1917 he published *Can the Bolsheviks' Retain State Power?* which directly took on the arguments of the right-wing parties who argued that the working class could not run society. Famously, he wrote *State and Revolution,* a book that explored the nature of the state, its origins and the need for the capitalist state to be smashed. *State and Revolution* developed Marx and Engels' writings on the state into a practical discussion of the tasks of the revolutionary movement in Russia.

Lenin argued that the capitalist state had to be smashed. Workers could not take over this state and use it in their interests; they had to create their own workers' state. Lenin emphasised that this could only happen through the power of a mass revolutionary workers' movement. For Marxists, a workers' revolution is one where the majority of the population takes power in the interests of the majority, and defends its new state from counter-revolutionary forces. A workers' state would not be a mirror of the capitalist state—it would be one where the majority ran in society in their own collective interests.

In *Can the Bolsheviks' Retain State Power?* Lenin pointed out that there were already millions of workers in Russia, "faithful to the ideal of the Socialist State" and by the "drawing in of the workers, the poor, to the daily work of the managing the State" the Revolution would be able to massively increase the "apparatus of government" in the interests of the majority. In a brilliant account of the difference between a capitalist state and a workers' state, Lenin describes how each state would evict people from the homes. The capitalist state, he points out, uses the police, bailiffs and court officials to evict a family who cannot pay their rent. In working class areas, Lenin shows that the capitalists rely on mass military force because the workers' would mobilise in huge numbers to stop the eviction. The capitalist state relies on force to implement its decisions.

A workers' state, by contrast, would be concerned with making sure that everyone had adequate housing, until more homes could be built. That might mean requisitioning the homes or rich people to house those without shelter. Lenin considers how this process might take place:

> The proletarian state has to forcibly move a very poor family into a rich man's flat. Let us suppose that our

squad of workers' militia is fifteen strong; two sailors, two soldiers, two class-conscious workers (of whom, let us suppose, only one is a member of our Party, or a sympathiser), one intellectual, and eight from the poor working people, of whom at least five must be women, domestic servants, unskilled labourers, and so forth. The squad arrives at the rich man's flat, inspects it and finds that it consists of five rooms occupied by two men and two women—"You must squeeze up a bit into two rooms this winter, citizens, and prepare two rooms for two families now living in cellars. Until the time, with the aid of engineers (you are an engineer, aren't you?), we have built good dwellings for everybody, you will have to squeeze up a little. Your telephone will serve ten families. This will save a hundred hours of work wasted on shopping, and so forth. Now in your family there are two unemployed persons who can perform light work: a citizeness fifty-five years of age and a citizen fourteen years of age. They will be on duty for three hours a day supervising the proper distribution of provisions for ten families and keeping the necessary account of this. The student citizen in our squad will now write out this state order in two copies and you will be kind enough to give us a signed declaration that you will faithfully carry it out".

Lenin concludes, that this "can illustrate how the distinction between the old bourgeois and the new socialist state apparatus and state administration could be illustrated."[300] For Lenin and the Bolsheviks' the workers' state is based on a fundamental difference with the capitalist state. Under capitalism a minority of people govern in the interests of the rich, but under a workers' state the masses govern in their own interests:

We demand an immediate break with the prejudiced view that only the rich, or officials chosen from rich

> families, are capable of administering the state, of performing the ordinary, everyday work of administration. We demand that training in the work of state administration be conducted by class-conscious workers and soldiers and that this training be begun at once, i.e., that a beginning be made at once in training all the working people, all the poor, for this work.[301]

But states are instruments of class rule, and this is also true of the workers' state. A successful seizure of power by the workers will not see the capitalist class disappear and give up. The generals, rich people and their politicians will still be there and will organise to try to regain their wealth and power, and the workers' state will have to defend itself, using force if necessary. This did happen after workers took power in Russia, when the old ruling class immediately tried to use military force to overthrow the soviets and workers' power. The Civil War, which saw imperialist armies from many different lands invade Russia, was the most brutal of attempts to regain control. Soviet power had to use the state they had created to defend the interests of the workers. This included organising armed resistance and putting together the Red Army.

In *State and Revolution*, Lenin emphasises the role of the new workers' state:

> The labouring people need a state only to suppress the resistance of the exploiters, and only the proletariat is in a position to direct this suppression, to carry it out; for the proletariat is the only class that is consistently revolutionary, the only class that can unite all the labouring and exploited people in the struggle against the bourgeoisie, in its complete overthrow.[302]

The seizure of power by the working class is only the first step in a process. Nonetheless, the critical juncture in a revolutionary process will be when the workers' movement is able to seize power. Insurrection, the actual seizure of power, is the crowning act of a revolution. The taking of power by the workers is the moment of transition between a capitalist state and a workers' state.

Insurrection is not the act of a small minority of revolutionaries. It is a mass collective act. In Russia, the Petrograd Soviet created a "Military Revolutionary Committee". This body was directly linked to Soviet power, as well as coordinating the revolutionary military forces. On 25 October 1917 [303] revolutionary workers and soldiers seized Petrograd's key infrastructure in the name of the Soviets, the workers organisation—bridges, telegraph and telephone buildings, post offices, banks and so on. With barely a shot fired and almost no casualties, the massed forces of the revolution took power.

That afternoon, Lenin came out of hiding, and spoke to the Petrograd Soviet:

> The oppressed themselves will form the government. The old state will be destroyed and a new administration created in the form of soviets. Now begins a new era in the history of Russia and this third Russian Revolution. One of our tasks is to end the war; for that capitalism must be conquered. In this we shall be helped by the world working class, which has already begun to develop in Italy, Germany and Britain. Within Russia an enormous section of the peasantry has said 'enough of fooling around with the capitalists; we will go with the workers'. We must set out at once on the construction of a proletarian, socialist state.[304]

When the Russian workers' and soldiers' councils took power it opened up the possibility for a fundamentally different way of organising society. But it was only the start of a transitional process. When Marx looked at the Paris Commune he saw the "political ascendancy" of the working class. As Draper explains, "Marx presented the Commune as a workers' government, as the political form of the transition to a new social order", but then cautions that "a 'working-class government' that lasted only 72 days can hardly be expected to clearly exhibit the expected historical characteristic of a workers' state". It was, rather, an "incipient" workers' state, in the process of being born.[305]

The Commune was, for Marx, a clear indication of the basic form of a workers' state, it was "the political form at last discovered under which to work out the economical emancipation of Labour". Crucially it was also the form discovered by the proletariat in revolt, not handed down by intellectuals from above. The Commune was the beginning of a process, not the end. As Marx says, "the Commune was, therefore, to serve as a lever for uprooting the economical foundations upon which rests the existence of classes, and therefore of class rule".[306]

They knew that its class enemies would assault a newly created workers' state from all sides. Thus, workers' power is first and foremost the idea that in the aftermath of a revolution, workers' need to use their class power to suppress the counter-revolution.

Marx celebrated the enormous expansion of democracy in the Paris Commune and noted the "antidemocratic character" of its enemies.[307] For Marx, a workers' state was about "smashing" the capitalist state and replacing it with a new system organised on the basis of mass democratic participation.

Democracy under capitalism is nothing more than democracy for the rich. To this, Lenin contrasts revolutionary democracy—an "immense expansion" of democracy "for the poor", but points out this will not come through piecemeal reforms because of the "resistance of the exploiter-capitalists".[308] Instead, it can only come through the workers' state.

Since a state only exists for one class to suppress another, once the enemies of the working class have been defeated, there will be no need for a workers' state. Revolutionary socialists are fighting for a society without classes. This means ending the separation between those who own and control the means of production and the majority who do the work. The workers' state is thus transitional—not the end goal. Marxists argue that once class differences disappear, the workers' state will wither away and disappear as workers begin to live their lives in a completely different way, without coercion or force. Lenin wrote:

> Only in communist society, when the resistance of the capitalists has been definitively crushed, when the capitalists have disappeared, when there are no classes... only then does 'the state... disappear' and does it 'become possible to speak of freedom'. Only then will a truly complete democracy, democracy without any exceptions whatever, become possible and be realised.[309]

Lenin is careful to avoid utopianism. He is not arguing that within a workers state there will be no disagreement or debate. Rather, as we will see, a workers' state would be filled with discussion about how to organise society. But he says that although there might still be "excesses" by individuals, he sees these as being solved through collective responses by the people—rather like a crowd intervenes to stop a scuffle in the street. But Lenin also argues that the workers' state will have begun to address the root causes of such "excesses":

> We know that the fundamental social causes of excesses which consist in the violation of the rules of social intercourse, is the exploitation of the masses, their want and their poverty. With the removal of this chief cause, excesses will inevitably begin to 'wither away'. We do not know with what speed and calibration; but we do know that they will all wither away. With their withering away the state will also wither away.[310]

The workers' state is simultaneously the armed organisation of the working class in defence of its victory, and the beginnings of a new society based on mass democracy, which will eventually see the withering away of the state completely.

It is important to be clear on one specific point here. When Marx, Engels and Lenin write about the "withering away" of the state, they mean the withering way and disappearance of the workers' state after a successful workers' revolution. Some on the left have tried to use Marx and Engels' arguments to suggest that the capitalist state could wither away without the revolutionary transition. As we have seen, the capitalist state exists to perpetuate the capitalist system. It will not disappear on its own. It must be destroyed and a workers' state created that can begin the transition to a classless society.

The end game for revolutionaries is not the permanent repression of the capitalist class—rather it is the end of class society. As Lenin continued, "The exploited classes need political rule in order completely to abolish all exploitation".[311] In the immediate aftermath of the seizure of power a workers' state will have a great deal to do to start to abolish all the inequalities, poverty and problems left by capitalist rule. The first task will be to protect the fledgling workers' state from capitalist counter-revolution. But this will not mean the neglecting of other tasks. In the immediate aftermath of the seizure of power in 1917 soviet power began to organise to tackle key social questions—redistributing land, addressing inequality and oppression, and nationalising the wealth of the former capitalist class.

Revolution today will also mean addressing poverty, inequality and oppression. The new workers' state will need to immediately address the environmental crisis. This will mean implementing an urgent program to reduce emissions and protect communities. It will require the shutting down of the fossil fuel multinationals, the seizure of their assets and the redistribution of wealth for use to build a sustainable infrastructure for a socialist society. Only a workers' state will be able to achieve this and that will require the working class taking control of society, running it in their interests and resisting the violence and terror of counter-revolution.

Once the enemies of a workers' state are defeated the workers' state will begin to disappear. The need for repressive institutions such as the police and courts will vanish as workers' power means that ordinary people are provided with decent wages, homes, food and other essentials. As Engels argued:

> The first act by virtue of which the [workers'] state really constitutes itself the representative of the whole of society—the taking possession of the means of production in the name of society—this is, at the same time, its last independent act as a state. State interference in social relations becomes, in one domain after another, superfluous, and then dies out of itself; the government of persons is replaced by the administration of things, and by the conduct of processes of production. The state is not 'abolished'. It dies out.[312]

Under capitalism, a tiny minority owns and controls the means of production. A workers' state would nationalise the infrastructure, banks, land and factories so that they can be controlled and used in the interests of all. The abolishment of private property and workers' control over the means of production would allow ordinary people to begin to address the legacy of capitalist destruction.

In the next chapter, we will discuss how a socialist society would democratically organise the economy in the interests of everyone and how this would work.

Chapter 9
The socialist alternative to capitalism

Imagining a functioning alternative to capitalism is part of the struggle against the system. Such visions can inspire and motivate activists. Radicals have often used fiction to explore these futures, at the same time as exposing the reality of capitalism itself. One famous example is William Morris' *News from Nowhere* (1890) which depicts a worker travelling forward in time to a socialist society where property is held in common, rivers are no longer polluted, people live fulfilling lives and the Houses of Parliament in London have been converted to a "dung market"!

The history of the radical movement has seen many activists, from many different traditions, who have tried to theorise how a society might be organised that rationally uses resources and human labour in everyone's interests. In some cases, those radicals have tried to create such societies—communes and utopian communities—based on collective ownership of property and democratic decision making.

The most radical group to come out of the English Revolution were the Diggers. The Diggers were led by Gerrard Winstanley, and in 1649, they set up a network of agrarian communes. The most famous of these was on St George's Hill in Surrey. The Diggers were quickly forced to abandon their communes as state repression and local landowners organised to expel them.

But in his pamphlet *The Law of Freedom* (1651) Winstanley was one of the earliest radicals to set out a detailed plan for how a society based on common ownership might function.[313] In Winstanley's vision, elected officers and overseers managed the functioning of society. A system of storehouses would be set up for manufactured goods and raw materials so that local producers could distribute the goods they made and take what was needed for their families.

Winstanley hoped his society could transform every aspect of peoples' lives, setting out plans for how the people would democratise the church, transform marriage and challenge gender inequality—though he still believed that only men should vote. His vision of society was utopian in the sense that it was not possible for it to be built in the context of English society at the end of the Civil War—in fact the suppression of the Diggers and other radicals of the period took place because Oliver Cromwell's government did not want to end private property. The central task for Winstanley was to come up with a plausible vision of how the equal distribution of materials, food and goods that people needed to survive would work. He imagined a network of local storehouses where the goods people made were stored for collection and awaited collection by those who needed them. The questions that Winstanley grappled with remain important today. How will we produce the essentials that people need in the most sustainable way?

Socialism will, first and foremost, be about satisfying the needs of humanity in the most sustainable and equitable way possible. This will require the planning of production, to ensure that society is producing the food, shelter, transport, housing, medical supplies and services that are needed, and doing it in a way that has the least impact upon the environment while ensuring everyone has access to what they need to live a fulsome life. A prerequisite for society to be able to democratically plan production is the control of the means of production—the factories, work places, infrastructure and land—by the working class. This means that the overthrow of capitalist relations are essential to the creation of such a society. In this chapter, we will look at how the planning of production might take place.

*

There are no pre-prepared plans, no blueprints, for the building of a socialist society. As Lenin wrote when considering the transition to a communist society from the socialist society introduced in the immediate aftermath of a workers' revolution: "We do not and cannot know by what stages, by what practical measures, humanity will proceed to this supreme aim." [314] But just as Marx, Engels and Lenin drew from the experience of the Paris Commune and other revolutions such as the 1905 Russian Revolution to inform their vision of socialism, we too must learn from the experience of revolutionary movements to help imagine a socialist world.

Capitalism is an anarchic system of production. A rational economy would be able to distribute goods, resources and services to all those that need them. Capitalism is unable to do this as it bases the allocation of resources on who can pay, not who has needs. Production is solely for profit. In contrast, socialists argue that planning will need to involve the mass participation of workers in decision making about production. This means we argue for *democratic planning*—but our vision of a planned economy is one that arises out of revolutionary change, rather than being imposed from above. The basis for such a society are the organisations that workers create during revolution.

Planning and the environment

In 1992 at the "Earth Summit" in Rio de Janeiro adopted the United Nations Framework Convention on Climate Change (UNFCCC). The supreme decision-making body of the UNFCCC is the Conference of the Parties "COP" which meets annually. As I have argued earlier, the COP process has been deeply flawed and failed to address the challenge of climate change. Yet for many people the annual meetings of the COP form a sort of world government on climate change, setting out frameworks and priorities to deal with ecological disaster.

In contrast to the impotence of the UNFCCC a socialist approach to the climate crisis would emphasise the role of local production units in tackling issues. Unlike under capitalism where governments hope that industries, organisations or workplaces will reduce their emissions in line with their targets, as an add-on to their normal activities, a socialist planned economy would see tackling climate change (and other ecological issues) as intrinsic to their day-to-day behaviour. Indeed a socialist world would prioritise action on the climate crisis, in contrast to capitalism, which fails to deploy resources and wealth to tackle the issue. Under socialism, addressing the ecological crisis would require immediate and priority use of resources and labour.

That said, there would need to be national and international coordination and organisation. Addressing the global inequality that has arisen out of the history of colonialism and imperialism would be a priority of a socialist society trying to address ecological crisis. Unlike the UNFCCC process, a socialist response to climate change would not try and separate climate change from wider questions of economic and political justice.

A global socialist society would share wealth and resources between areas of the world, to help countries that had been underdeveloped by capitalism deal with the environmental crisis and in order that they could develop sustainably. Under a socialist society, where the profit motive has been removed, there would be no reason for one part of the world to hoard wealth and resources when it was desperately needed elsewhere. Sharing resources like this can be contrasted to the "aid" that rich nations give to poorer countries under capitalism—aid that comes with strings attached.

Imagine how we might begin to address the problem of climate change if we were not constrained by capitalism's interests and we incorporated workers into the process at every level. A system of global conferences where scientists and delegates from every part of the world came up with world plans to allocate resources and wealth to deal with climate crisis. At the same time, these conferences would come up with an international framework to reduce emissions. Unlike the flawed COP process, this would not be shaped by the interests of competing capitalist states, but by the needs of ordinary people. From such agreements, each area of the world would have its own emissions reduction targets, but these would be set based on science, rather than voluntary proposals from nation-states.

In each part of the world, a central council, based on elected delegates from regional workers' councils, industries and economic sectors, would discuss the plans and targets. Because this would involve representatives from different cities, towns, industries and workplaces, they could input the needs of their communities and workforces as well as offer plans and strategies based on that knowledge. These meetings would agree priorities, allocate resources and make decisions—but crucially these agreements would be the result of the coming together of an international framework and information from below.

The input from workers would be crucial. There would be no point in making a national agreement about energy generation, for instance, without input from workers in the energy sector who could bring their own ideas and concerns. Yet this is precisely what does happen under capitalism. Today, every worker knows what it is like when senior management impose a plan from above without consulting those who have to do the work. This is why genuine workers' democracy is so important to economic planning.

Under socialism workers in every locality, every office, factory, workplace and community would be able to discuss and debate their contribution to dealing with climate change (and every other political and economic issue). This might mean ideas on how to reduce energy use, how to change machinery to reduce pollution, how to redesign buildings and offices to make them more sustainable. Transport workers would be involved in redesigning public transport to eliminate individual car usage and increase usage of buses, trams and trains. City or town councils would co-ordinate these plans with decisions about the siting of houses, workplaces, hospitals and schools. The latest technology could be utilised and made available to reduce energy wasted through needless travel. Unsustainable international business travel would be outdated as online conferences replace such meetings. It is always striking how enthusiastic workers are when they imagine redesigning their towns, communities and workplaces in the interest of people and planet. Under capitalism ordinary people have no say in such decision-making process. Under socialism, the enthusiasm would be unleashed.

The idea that under socialism we could bring together international frameworks for dealing with climate change, and mass participation in the planning of workplaces, cities and the wider economy, gives us a glimpse of how we could address the climate crisis.

Such a system could also address the legacy of global inequality. Capitalism's division of the world into different nation-states would gradually break down over time under socialism. Borders only exist in order to protect the national interests of different capitalist economies. A socialist society would welcome, indeed encourage, the movement of people fleeing natural disasters or climate change. However, a socialist society would also not see borders as barriers for sharing resources. The most obvious example of this might be the way that hotter areas of the world could provide solar generated energy to the rest of the globe. In the short-term, this might require compensation, or the movement of resources reciprocally between parts of the world. In the longer-term, the idea of refusing renewable energy to one part of the world simply because it is on the other side of a line drawn on a map would seem archaic. After all, carbon dioxide knows no borders.

A global socialist society would coordinate and plan both to deal with climate change and to respond to the disasters that are inevitable because of historic emissions. While it is true that even under capitalism, governments share resources for example fighting wildfires, the scale of recent wildfires has been such that spare equipment is not available. Planning production rationally and democratically would allow resources to be released to make sure enough equipment, experience and technology is available when disaster hits. A socialist society would not be churning out SUVs from car plants when the world is crying out for more fire-fighting equipment.

The ability to rationally deploy resources would mean other ecological problems could be curtailed or prevented. A rational agriculture would require regional and global coordination—but it would also share best practices. Local producers, indigenous peoples and peasant farmers around the world have the knowledge about how to produce food sustainably and with the least impact on the wider environment. Socialism would allow those producers to share and learn from each other, rather than producing the crop that maximises profit.

In the *Communist Manifesto*, Marx and Engels argued for the "gradual abolition of all the distinction between town and country by a more equable distribution of the populace over the country".[315] In this they were responding to a contemporary manifestation of ecological crisis—the breakdown in rural economies and environment through the concentration of population and resources in urban areas. In particular, Marx and Engels later saw that the large urban areas directly led to the degradation of the rural environment, particularly the soil, as nutrients that entered crops were taken to the cities and never returned to the countryside.[316]

As John Bellamy Foster has written, "What made the division between town and country under capitalism so acute was the uncontrolled industrialization, concentration of capital, and concomitant effects on cities like London and Manchester".[317] The hope that a future society might abolish the distinction between the two was a reaction to the particularly odious nature of capitalist cities and their destruction of people and planet. But it was much more than a "return to nature" idea. William Morris, in calling for the abolition of the division between town and country was not arguing to remove urban areas entirely, rather he was imagining how towns and cities might be reconstructed in more sustainable ways. Foster says: "Although Morris admired the countryside, what he continually sought, as expressed in *News from Nowhere* and elsewhere, was not a retreat to some abstract nature, but a much more complex, dialectical integration of town and country".[318]

Foster continues:

> If the pivotal change in Morris's revolutionary utopia is the transformation of alienated mechanical labor into unalienated artistic labor, its overarching manifestation is the metamorphosis of town and country, standing for the new relation to the earth, no longer the object of mere conquest. In the beginning of the new epoch, townspeople had dispersed into the countryside, causing much disruption, but eventually a new equilibrium was created.[319]

We should be wary of seeing the world portrayed in Morris's *News from Nowhere* as a blueprint for a future communist world. In it however, we can see a vision of a world where the profit motive has given way to a new way of thinking that places the relationship between human society and wider nature at the heart of its daily economic behaviour. Central to this will be the participation of ordinary people in organising their society.

Of course, democratic planning like this is not just restricted to the environment. Imagine how such a framework might have been used to respond to the Coronavirus pandemic—sharing resources and knowledge between scientific institutions and countries. Shifting resources between areas of the world at particular points and making sure medical knowledge was freely available. Contrast this with how the world did respond—with wealthy nations hoarding vaccines and pharmaceutical companies producing vaccines for profit.

Under capitalism, in every workplace, workers know how their jobs could better contribute to society. But because production is made in the interest of profit, we never have a say in those decisions. The world needs more ambulances, fire-engines, trains and trams, yet capitalist logic has the world producing tanks, military aircraft and automobiles. Placing workers at the heart of planning the economy will allow the rational use of resources in the interest of everyone and our planet.

*

Before looking at how democratic planning might work in more detail, it is worth briefly examining other examples of economic planning. The first is the planning that takes place within capitalism itself. This occurs either when individual companies plan their own production, or when nation-states gear their economy toward a specific national outcome. The second example is the top-down, command control of the economy, which characterised the Soviet Union and Eastern bloc countries. Both examples subordinate the interests and labour of workers' to interests other than their own. After looking at these examples this chapter will conclude with a discussion of the mass democratic planning of the economy that would characterise a socialist society.

Planning under capitalism

Capitalism is able, when required, to coordinate production to solve particular issues. Indeed modern multinationals, organising production through global networks of supply chains and "just in time" production, have to plan production in many ways—coordinating labour, resources and raw materials. This is planning to maximise profit not to satisfy human needs.

Similarly at times, whole states have proven capable of organising national production in order to solve specific issues—most obviously during wartime. In the Second World War, all the belligerent states used forms of economic planning to run the wartime economy. Britain, restricted by blockades and bombing, centrally coordinated the feeding of its population, and military production. Left economist Pat Devine, explains that they did this using the "allocation of 'manpower'".[320]

While wartime planning like this was successful, it did not address inequality or benefit everyone equally. Indeed the model itself was designed to allow the continued functioning of a capitalist economy insofar as possible under wartime conditions.[321] "On average", many people simply lost out, as standards of living fell, though the population "were healthier than ever before".[322] Wartime planning like this was, in this respect, no different to the economic planning that firms make when trying to maximise profit—the allocation of resources towards specific ends.

Nonetheless, the success of centralised planning in the allocation of resources to specific industries demonstrates its superiority as a method of organising the economy compared to, say, the free market. Direct allocation of resources driven by a government plan can have remarkable short-term successes. In 1961 the US had not yet placed an astronaut in orbit around the Earth, yet President Kennedy was confident enough about the US economy's potential to direct the country to place a "man on the moon" before "the decade was out" something the US achieved in July 1969. That the US could do this, at the same time as fighting the war in Vietnam, is testament to the potential of centralised planning even under capitalism. But the fact that the US did this at a time of enormous poverty, inequality and political turmoil also shows that under capitalism direction of resources to solve particular problems can be done, but it will always take place in the interests of that society not those of the whole population.

Citizen Assemblies: helping to plan capitalism?

Could capitalism be changed? Some activists argue that the participation of ordinary people will be enough to change how capitalism behaves. This neglects how production under capitalism arises out of capital's desire to maximise profit, and forms of democratic participation that fail to challenge the dynamic of capitalist production will have limited, if any, success.

For instance some activists, notably Extinction Rebellion (XR), have recently raised the idea of "citizens' assemblies" (CAs). In this model of democracy groups of randomly selected individuals form an assembly to discuss specific issues and come up with recommendations. XR argue that CAs "will empower citizens to actually work together and take responsibility for our climate and ecological emergency".

There is no doubt that CAs can allow groups of people to take part in complex debates about particular issues. The objection to these as a model for an alternative democracy is not that randomly selected groups of people cannot come to informed choices through a process of debate and discussion. The problem is that CAs have no control over production—they cannot implement any decisions because there is no collective ownership of the means of production. This model of CAs abstracts democracy from wider economic and political forces in society. In this, CAs have much in common with the idea of "demarchy" formulated by John Burnheim. In criticising "demarchy", Devine makes the point that such approaches are not actually very democratic as they avoid "generalised participation".[323] In addition, those who make the decisions have no accountability to wider society, and no requirement for the capitalists to implement these decisions. In fact, such models are less democratic than some forms of parliamentary democracy.

If we recall Marx's celebration of the democratic process central to the Paris Commune it was down to both the participation of the electorate and the accountability of those elected through instantaneous recall. The Commune also brought together the "executive and legislative" sides of state rule. But crucial to the functioning of the Commune was its formation. The Commune was created by revolution—the democratic institutions central to the Commune were made by the masses. Thus electors participating in debates and elections were participating in their own institutions, and organising society in their own interests.

Real democratic economic planning can only come from the producers themselves owning and controlling production.

State capitalist planning

Another model of planning is that which arose in Russia after the defeat of the revolution and emulated in Eastern Europe, following the defeat of Nazi Germany, when Red Army tanks set up regimes pliant towards the Soviet Union. The isolation and defeat of the Russian Revolution saw the destruction of any workers' control over production. Under Stalin, the state bureaucracy developed into a ruling class that managed a highly centralised top down "command economy". This state capitalist society was organised not in the interests of the mass of the population, but the ruling bureaucracy. Nonetheless, as with the capitalist nations, it was able to achieve significant economic development, as well as developing its own nuclear arms programme.[324] Crucially however state capitalism did this through heavy repression and exploitation of the working class and peasantry. Writing in 1989 about what he calls the "statist" countries, Devine argued that:

> The administrative command planning system, based on vertical flows of information and instructions, lubricated by vertical and horizontal bargaining and negotiation within the ruling bureaucracy, is generally accepted as having impressive achievements to its credit... It has been the vehicle for rapid economic growth and regional development, maintained full employment and low rates of inflation, and has been associated with some increase in standards of living and cultural development. It has also coexisted with appalling repression and violation of individual freedom and been the vehicle for arbitrary decision-making, inefficiency and waste, endemic shortage and lack of consumer satisfaction.[325]

The state capitalist Soviet Union, and the client states it created in Eastern Europe were locked into imperialist conflict with the Western economies, particularly the US. While the rhetoric of these governments used the label of socialism, the logic of their economies was driven by competition with the West, primarily the arms race. As such, the needs of ordinary people were subordinated to the collective interests of the ruling bureaucratic class as they accumulated wealth in competition with the Western powers.

The command economies produced central economic targets epitomised by the various "Five Year Plans". Within these however there was no freedom for the workers in industries, or workplaces to shape the plan. Devine notes that rather than production targets being assigned to direct sections of the economy they were actually used as a "basis for rewarding or penalizing enterprises, their managers and their workers". In other words, rather than the top-down "plan" being about creating a framework for wider production, it was a method of encouraging workers to produce in a particular way, not involving workers in those decisions.[326]

A planned economy that acts in the interest of the whole population, while simultaneously being able to deal with threats such as ecological disaster in a way that does not penalise one group of people, or one geographical region, over another, will require the maximum participation of the "associated producers" at every level of its functioning. How might this work in practice, and what can we learn from previous experiences?

Is market socialism an alternative?

Because state capitalist regimes ruled using the language of socialism, their top-down economies have become synonymous for many bourgeois economists with actual socialism. Some on the left reject the idea of democratic planning, arguing for a blend of free market and state capitalism. Such "market socialism" was associated in particular with the academic Alec Nove, but Nove's system still relied on the profit motive to encourage individual units of production.[327] For Nove "market socialism" still required the profit motive for individual production units.

Callinicos points out that the problem is that in a competitive market, "the allocation of resources is the unintended outcome of competition between the firms that jointly but not collectively control the economy".[328] Like any other capitalist market, for companies to survive they have to reduce costs, which means attacking workers' conditions—either by making them work harder, or cutting their wages. This means that even if the workers run a company under "market socialism" they are trapped by capitalist logic. This is a reason that workers' co-operatives have to make difficult choices—the logic of the market applies to them as much as any other firm.

Callinicos concludes:

> The logic of a market economy therefore tends to undermine and eventually to overwhelm any islands of democracy and equality that may emerge within it. This means that socialists... who believe that it is possible to democratise the market, tend to face a dilemma of their own. Either they impose all sorts of restrictions on the functioning of the market to prevent it from eroding democracy, in which case any economy based on the principles they propose is likely to break down because they prevent the logic of competition from operating properly, or, if they try to ensure this logic will operate, it will destroy the socialist ideals they are trying to realise.

How democratic planning might work

Genuine socialist democratic planning can only come out of the mass involvement of workers in the decisions taken about the production process itself. This is why revolution is a prerequisite for the establishment of a genuine democratic planned economy. Workers' involvement in the revolutionary process creates the organisations that will form the basis of the new economic decision making process. In Russia these workers' councils or Soviets were initially bodies created by workers to organise their revolutionary struggle, but they quickly evolved into organs of workers' control. The workers' insurrection in October 1917 was the seizure of power that created a workers' state and saw the working class take ownership of the "means of production"—the factories, workplaces, land and infrastructure—from the capitalist class.

A democratically-planned economy means placing workers' democracy central to every stage of the economic process. We have already discussed how this might work, with for dealing with climate change. An international framework for emissions reductions would be combined with information from individual production units, industries and workplaces shaping national contributions to the global framework.

A similar process would need to take place in every part of the economy. Global, national and regional needs would lead to a broad requirement for resources and products. This broad outline would be communicated to the relevant workplaces—which would then produce products along the general lines of the agreed plan. It is important to note that these production plans would be both specific—in terms of the types of goods produced—and general in the sense of creating a framework for what type of resource or product was needed. For instance, a plan for a specific region might say that a certain amount of people would need to be able to travel by public transport. Within this general framework, a local city transport plan might call for the use of trams, not buses. Such a decision would be the result of intense discussion involving input from the people of different communities, workplaces and other public services. Once such a decision was agreed, it would then mean that all the affected institutions and workplaces would have to frame their productive activity through the filter of this agreement. It would determine what materials were needed, which machinery was obtained and what energy infrastructure would be needed. Again, the input of workers in other areas of the economy about availability of resources or labour would help determine what was agreed.

Such plans can only be made by ensuring workers are central to decisions at every level. There is no point having a central plan if workers know they cannot produce what is needed. Information on resources, energy, productive capacity and labour availability would need to be constantly passed up and down the networks. But because economies are not just hierarchical, this information would also need to be passed horizontally, between production units. Under capitalism, a car manufacturer relies on dozens of other firms to supply components, materials and energy. But under capitalism these relationships exist on the basis of profit. Under a socialist society, a production unit would also need these networks, but there would be a sharing of information and resources to ensure that production was coordinated—to reduce waste and make sure that production satisfied needs.

The model of workers' democracy that can arise in revolutionary situations, with workers electing a council to debate and plan their activity, would need to be expanded into a national structure. In the Russian revolution, workers in particular workplaces elected delegates to their workplace council. Those councils then elected representatives to city-wide bodies, and these bodies would send representation to national Soviets. Such a model ensures that each decision-making body retains a link to the workplace and the knowledge and interests of the workers there. This does not preclude other bodies being set up—there might be local bodies representing medical workers for instance, or national organisations for particular types of workers. These institutions would enable different professions to share knowledge. Think of how scientists might share information to national and international bodies about latest advances. In the Russian revolution local communities set up Soviets to ensure their needs and concerns were part of wider political debates. In a socialist society, local communities would similarly elect representatives to any bodies whose decisions might affect them.

One model for such a democratic planned economy is that proposed by Devine, who calls it "negotiated coordination", arguing that each production unit would be constantly sharing information and knowledge "to arrive through negotiation at a definition of the social interest in relation to current production and the type and distribution of investment".[329] For Devine this means "overall priorities" are assigned, arising from inputs from every area of the economy, but such broad frameworks give plenty of leeway for local decisions and agreements.

Crucially such a system, which emphasises decentralised, localised production, within a national framework, would rely on different production units passing up information on needs and resources and the outcomes of earlier discussions. Lower bodies would elect individuals to higher bodies so that those groups were informed by experiences in the wider economy as well as being accountable to them. The highest bodies would use information available to them to set a framework, and the broadest priorities which are then passed back down to other institutions for implementation.

Actual production decisions would rest, not at the highest level, but in the realm of the workers in the production units that would be carrying out the work. This means that every production unit would make decisions, and engage in production, based not on self-interested profit making, but within the framework set by a national coordinating body, and informed about wider factors—particularly ecological ones.

The constant passing of information upwards and downwards is, as Devine argues, vertical but not hierarchical. There would need to be a great deal of horizontal discussions too, sharing information, planning, coordinating and organising. The organising of production in this way would, no doubt, lead to plenty of meetings and debates. Though unlike under capitalism, where meetings are a chore that swell to fill the working day, a socialist society would see participation by people who saw the planned economy as theirs, and thus had a vested interest in making it a success.

This presentation of how a democratically-planned economy might work out is deliberately broad. It is important to emphasise the way that coordination and negotiation between different bodies would allow society to produce what was needed within a wider framework, one based on sustainability and the need to satisfy human needs. There can be no blueprint for how a future society will be organised. Those who make the revolution and create a new socialist society will know best how to make decisions and organise production. There is no doubt that they will experiment with different models and ideas. The important thing is that because there would no longer be a division between classes, production decisions would no longer be made by a minority in pursuit of profit. Instead, under socialism, such decisions will be made by the majority of society in their own interests, Under capitalism workers have no say in how production is organised, or what is manufactured. In a socialist society the producers would be given the freedom to shape their economy and how it functioned.

Information technology and planning

Bourgeoisie economists argue that the free market is the only way to organise society, because prices of goods and services send signals to producers about what to make. But since there are millions of hungry, homeless or jobless people the capitalist market clearly does not function to satisfy need. Overproduction of some goods, while there are shortages of others arise not because of the wrong price signals, but because capitalists are hungry for profit. However, capitalism has produced technologies that can help facilitate a rational economy. We should take it as read that a socialist society would use, and develop, technologies that improve communication, data analysis and so on. Recently, some thinkers have explored how information technology can do more than this, and "provide efficient methods of social coordination in environments where price signals are missing".[330] Evgeny Morozov, explains that critics of planning have argued it cannot work because of a lack of "real-time insights into the shifting tastes of consumers".[331] Today, information technology offers insights into patterns of consumption that could not have been comprehended a few years ago.

As more and more people order services and shop online, retailers like Amazon and social media providers have developed complex software whose algorithms can make predictions and needs. Many readers will know the phenomena—you order a particular product from a supermarket, and you get an email advertising something else that you might like. These retailers use it to encourage further purchases, but Morozov suggests that "'feedback infrastructure' can foresee and facilitate the satisfaction of our needs in ways unimaginable to central planners." He points out "such predictive capacity is a function, not of the mysterious working of the price system, but of the data held by platforms".[332]

Another radical economist Daniel Saros has argued that a decentralised, planned economy could use a "central catalogue" of products, containing the details of products made by different producers, which can be ordered by consumers using a unique card. This would allow them to register needs in advance (while not preventing them ordering goods later) of a specific production cycle and help producers plan what is needed. He envisages a system where the needs input by different consumers are linked to data analysis of trends and patterns to help allocate resources and plan production. Crucially this sort of model does not take away from the decision-making role of groups of workers. But it shows that information technology could help rationally organise production through the analysis of vast amounts of data.[333]

Consider the vast amount of data that social media companies and online retailers know about us—data about everything from our current physical location to the addresses of our home and workplace, our historic buying habits, interests and preferences. Today this data is used to get us to consume more in the interest of profit. A rational society could use this data to help plan production, to ensure resources are allocated to where they are needed and help make sure fair use of resources.

Morozov goes further and argues that information technology could also help "flag social problems and even to facilitate deliberation around them", and match groups who needed problems solved with those who had skills or knowledge that could help. Crucially though he points out that "assuming this takes place outside the commercial realm, there would be no barriers, such as patents, to impede the sharing of knowledge".[334] Under capitalism, technology—digital or otherwise—is subordinated to the drive to make profit. A socialist society would free up enormous potential to use such technology to satisfy need and rationally allocate labour and resources.

Socialism and democratic participation

When socialists discuss how a democratically planned economy might work, we can draw on the experience of workers' in revolution. Workers' struggle requires coordinating and planning at every level. Even organising a small picket line requires workers to discuss times, locations and plan rotas—as well as organising refreshments and banners. Accounts of historic revolutions show that during such upheavals workers have to organise and coordinate on a massive scale. The debates are wide-ranging and often intense. A great example of this comes from the Hungarian Revolution of 1956. In Hungary, a workers' revolution took place against the government's pro-Soviet policies. The revolution saw mass protests, the arming of workers, and the creation of workers' councils to co-ordinate the revolution.[335] Socialist journalist Peter Fryer's eyewitness account gives a sense of the workers' councils:

> In their spontaneous origin, in their composition, in their sense of responsibility, in their efficient organisation of food supplies and civil order, in the restraint they exercised on the wild elements among the youth, in the wisdom with which so many of them handled the problem of Soviet troops. And, not least, in their striking resemblance to the workers, peasants, and soldiers' councils which sprang up in Russia in the 1905 revolution and in February 1917, these committees,

> a network of which now extended over the whole of Hungary, were remarkably uniform.
>
> They were at once organs of insurrection—the coming together of delegates elected by factories and universities, mines and army units—and organs of popular self-government which the armed people trusted. Of course, as in every real revolution "from below" there was "too much" talking, arguing, bickering, coming and going, froth, excitement, agitation, ferment. This is one side of the picture. The other is the emergence to leading positions of ordinary men, women and youths, whom the AVH [the political police] domination had submerged. The revolution thrust them forward, aroused their civic pride and latent genius for organisation, set them to work to build democracy out of the ruins of bureaucracy.[336]

Fryer's honest reporting from Hungary for the British Communist Party's *Daily Worker* in 1956, saw his reports suppressed. They demonstrated the reality of state capitalism, contrasted with the living experience of revolution, where bureaucracy and hierarchy did not triumph over the experience of ordinary people. Fryer's account is of a workers' organisation at the height of revolution, where urgent pressures are placing immediate demands on a working class in revolt. Yet it also gives a sense of the coordination of different bodies, solving needs and organising the economy, emblematic of the "production units" at the heart of Pat Devine's portrayal of a functioning socialist society.

What Fryer's account also shows is that the revolutionary process, which puts in place the workers' councils that can form the basis for a democratic planned economy, would transform the people who organise them. Devine makes it clear that such an economy could only function if those participating broke with the atomised self-interest imposed on workers by capitalism:

> Unlike coordination through the coercion of market forces or state direction, negotiated coordination requires people to engage consciously with their interdependence and the consequences of their actions for others. It encourages people to transcend their sectional interests and take account also of the situation of others. It promotes cooperation on the basis of equality, mutual respect and a sense of community.
>
> Participation in the detailed construction of the social interest, taking account of the interests of all involved, is a central part of the process through which people cease to be objects, to be manipulated by administrative command or economic incentives, and become self-activating subjects who do what they do because they think it is right... narrow self-interest gives way to a broader self-interest, in which people's own interests are redefined to include the interest of others.[337]

For such a transformation to take place requires a society where the formal equality of bourgeois society ("we are all equal") is supplemented by real equality, socially and economically, which can only take place with the abolition of class society. It also requires the "abolition of the social division of labour". This means that everyone, irrespective of their work, will play a wider role in society. While the specialised knowledge of, say medical doctors, or telecoms engineers, would remain important those individuals could also play a role in other aspects of the economy—helping with childcare, taking part in local bodies' economic planning, or even on occasion working in entirely different sectors of the economy. The freeing up of resources, the creation of jobs and free education for all, would mean there would be no shortages of key workers and thus more time and energy for workers to do other things.

Throughout their lives, women and men have different needs and desires, based on their interests, circumstances, health and so on. There is no reason why someone who becomes a computer programmer at the age of 20 should remain working in the IT industry for their whole life. Indeed one of the problems of capitalism is the compartmentalisation of knowledge that takes place within workplaces, industries and sectors. In the context of a democratically planned economy, the active participation of individuals in different parts of the economy would help inform the decisions of that section. A health worker who spends time working in a factory may gain insights into the needs of workers there just as much as a worker from a manufacturing plant might learn from time spent working in a hospital.[338]

Such an approach to work is also a response to those who try to dismiss socialism with the crude question "who would clean toilets under socialism?" One answer might be that a future socialist society would give workers' who are doing unpleasant tasks rewards, perhaps in the form of extra time off. Another, and better, response might be that "everyone" would clean the toilets as part of their regular working life, seeing it as a contribution to the wider needs of society that enables it to function properly.

Under capitalism, workers are alienated from their labour, each other and the wider world. Society is structured in such a way that our labour is not our own—it belongs to the capitalist. We are dehumanised by the capitalist system of production and separated from each other. The products of labour—the goods we make or the services we provide—are not our own, they belong to the capitalist. The very thing that makes us human, our ability to labour and change the natural world to satisfy human need, is taken from us by the capitalist and ends up being turned against us.

The process of revolution will transform all the social relations we are part of. Over time, the transition to a fully socialist society will see work transformed—not just in terms of what workers make and do, but also in terms of how we have control over our work and the productions of our labour.

This means a break with bourgeois thought around what

constitutes work, and how it is organised. Marx made a similar argument:

> In a higher phase of communist society, after the enslaving subordination of the individual to the division of labour, and therewith also the antithesis between mental and physical labour, has vanished; after labour has become not only a means of life but life's prime want; after the productive forces have also increased with the all-around development of the individual, and all the springs of co-operative wealth flow more abundantly—only then can the narrow horizon of bourgeois right be crossed in its entirety and society inscribe on its banners: From each according to his ability, to each according to his needs![339]

Here Marx is distinguishing between the two stages of a socialist society. In the aftermath of a revolution, a new world is beginning to be constructed but such a society would bear the imprint of the capitalist world which preceded it. In the days, weeks and months after the overthrow of capitalism there would still be a fossil fuel industry and climate crisis, schools and hospitals in need of resources after being deprived of funds for so long, and there would still be a grossly unequal distribution of wealth and resources around the world. The task of this society would be firstly to protect itself from external, counter-revolutionary threats, and to begin constructing a rational society along the lines of one based on "negotiated coordination" described above.

In this "lower" stage of socialism workers would have to deal with the legacy of capitalism. This society would need to make decisions about production according to the needs of people, the dismantling of capitalism's fossil fuel infrastructure and a transition to a sustainable economy, and increasingly likely, about setting aside resources to deal with the consequences of climate disaster.

Once these immediate problems have been tackled, and society has begun moving towards a "higher stage", a much greater abundance of resources would be available to satisfy human needs. But society would still need to plan its interaction with the natural world. Even a future communist society cannot ignore the "planetary boundaries" which must constrain human activity or risk irreversible ecological damage. [340]

Marx argued that in the "higher" stage of socialism, society would be governed by the principle "from each according to his ability, to each according to his needs". These needs however, are not without constraint—social and ecological limits would still determine limits. As Norman Geras has said, "needs" would be judged against "some standard… which, large and generous as it may be possible for it to be, still falls short of any fantasy of abundance without limits".[341]

In his conception of a future communist society, Marx placed these concerns central to his argument:

> Freedom in this field can only consist in socialised man, the associated producers, rationally regulating their interchange with Nature, bringing it under their common control, instead of being ruled by it as by the blind forces of Nature; and achieving this with the least expenditure of energy and under conditions most favourable to, and worthy of, their human nature. But it nonetheless still remains a realm of necessity. Beyond it begins that development of human energy which is an end in itself, the true realm of freedom, which, however, can blossom forth only with this realm of necessity as its basis.[342]

How we can get to a society that can satisfy human need like this in a sustainable way, is the subject of the final chapter.

Chapter 10
The actuality of revolution

Capitalism has created a world of war, ecological disaster and economic crisis. It is a world of stark inequality where vast amounts of wealth are concentrated in the hands of a tiny number of people while billions of people do not have clean water, adequate food, affordable energy, decent homes or jobs that pay an adequate wage. At the same time, the logic of capitalism drives society to the brink of annihilation. The need for capital to accumulate creates the competition that drives countries, into competition with each other. Putin's invasion of Ukraine in response to Nato expansion is just one example of that, but it is an example that threatens nuclear conflict—a confrontation that would almost certainly end life on Earth.

Capital accumulation also drives the destruction of the natural world—transforming the relatively stable environment of the Holocene into the unpredictable and dangerous Anthropocene: an epoch of environmental and biodiversity crises. Capitalist production is also encouraging the emergence of new diseases. The likely origin of Covid-19 in systems of agriculture that concentrate animals and rely on monocultures is the most recent example of this. History and biology show that there is every possibility that future diseases may emerge and be even more lethal. The main response to this conjunction of capitalist crises is a rise in the politics of authoritarianism and the far right. Right wing governments from Britain to Australia have tried to divert attention from their failings through a combination of attacks on peoples' rights and an increase in oppression—particularly racism and anti-refugee policies, as well as an assault on women's and LGBT+ rights.

These crises can seem overwhelming. Given the scale of the threat to human existence, it is easy to respond with despair or apathy. In the face of disaster, we must offer hope—and that means discussing the actuality of revolution.

In 1924, just after the death of Lenin, the Hungarian Marxist Georg Lukács wrote a short book on Lenin's revolutionary ideas. Lukács made the point that it was the *potential* for revolution that motivated Lenin's theory and practice, even if revolution was not on the immediate agenda:

> For historical materialism as the conceptual expression of the proletariat's struggle for liberation could only be conceived and formulated theoretically when revolution was already on the historical agenda as a practical reality; when, in the misery of the proletariat, in Marx's words, was to be seen not only the misery itself but also the revolutionary element 'which will bring down the old order'.[343]

Lukács continued:

> The actuality of the revolution therefore implies study of each individual daily problem in concrete association with the socio-historic whole, as moments in the liberation of the proletariat. The development which Marxism thus underwent through Lenin consists merely—merely!—in its increasing grasp of the intimate, visible, and momentous connection between individual actions and general destiny—the revolutionary destiny of the whole working class. It merely means that every question of the day—precisely as a question of the day—at the same time became a fundamental problem of the revolution. [344]

This does not mean that Lenin thought that revolution could be willed into existence by revolutionaries. Rather, he understood that the nature of capitalism meant that revolution was possible and that revolutionaries should organise towards that reality.

Lenin argued that a revolutionary situation could develop under three conditions. Firstly, the ruling classes could no longer maintain their rule without change, while the lower classes were "unwilling to live in the old way"; secondly, the lower classes' suffering was worse than normal, and finally the masses who would not normally protest, were "drawn both by all the circumstances of the crisis and by the 'upper classes' themselves into independent historical action".[345]

What does revolution mean in the 21st century? As has been argued throughout this book, the alternative to capitalism is socialism, a society based on the replacement of the capitalist mode of production with a new economy, organised on the basis of workers' control and democratic planning.

The prerequisite for this is workers' power. This requires a workers' revolution against capitalism, the destruction of the capitalist state and its temporary replacement with a workers' state that will eventually "wither away" when humanity makes the transition to the "true realm of freedom".[346] Draper makes the point that in arguing this, in "presenting the proletariat as the ruling class to be", Marx argued that the working class "would only be doing what other classes had done before it" in overthrowing the old order to replace it with their own. The capitalist class itself had come to power through overthrowing the old, feudal order. A key difference for Marx, stresses Draper, is that unlike the capitalist class which grew up under feudalism, the working class cannot build up its economic power within capitalism.[347]

Workers, by definition, have no property. They do not own and control the means of production, so:

> [The working class] cannot inseminate its own system of economic power within the old one, thereby establishing a plateau of power from which to gain the

> political heights. The order necessarily is the reverse. The proletariat... must first conquer political power and then begin the process of socioeconomic transformation... For the proletariat, political power is needed as the engine with which to bring a new social order into existence".[348]

This is why socialist revolution is not an inevitability. But revolutionary situations *are* inevitable, precisely because capitalism is a system of exploitation. Revolutionaries cannot create the revolution, but they can organise towards the revolution—indeed this, Lukács argues, was the very essence of Lenin's practice. Specifically this means that revolutionaries must encourage every struggle, even those that are not yet revolutionary.

Capitalists will always try to extract more surplus value from workers, driving workers into conflict with it. This occurs whether or not workers have revolutionary ideas. The objective reality of capitalism means that bosses will try and exploit their workers more, forcing workers to resist. In resisting capitalism workers can generalise their experience and can encourage further struggles.

Because struggles take place in the context of capitalism, they all raise questions about the system itself. A strike by trade unionists for an above inflation pay rise poses wider questions about the wages system itself. This is why picket lines are often intensely political, even when the strike is purely over economic demands. LGBT+ protests might begin over specific issues—a demand for equal rights, or against specific instances of oppression—but they also contain a direct challenge to the capitalist "norm" of the bourgeois family. Black Lives Matter began as a roar of anger against police racism and killings, but rapidly developed into a movement that challenged the history of "racial capitalism" and the legacy of colonialism and slavery. Sometimes workers' might take action that is not directly about their own economic position. This might mean striking in solidarity with other groups of workers or over political issues—such as opposing specific government policies. In taking action like this, workers can also generalise about their own economic position. The key point is that struggle can encourage further struggle and leads to workers raising wider political issues.

In such struggles there are short term gains to be won—a proper pay rise, shorter hours, recognition of LGBT+ rights, or the imprisonment of police officers for racist killings. Longer term each of these struggles encourages the confidence and combativity of the working class as a whole.

Crucially however, revolutionaries need to argue for social movements to involve the organised working class. This means more than just involving individual workers—most activists and campaigners are workers, or are from the working class. Socialists want to involve workers as workers, not just as participants.

Because of their role in capitalist production, workers have enormous strength as well as being the class with the power to end capitalism itself. Their collective involvement in wider campaigns strengthens those campaigns. The power of workers, organised at the point of production, is a social force which makes the capitalist class wary—because if they use their strength they can stop the flow of profits. Social movements can win without the involvement of the organised working class. However, when workers are involved *en masse*, it can transform things.

In 1979, Tory MP John Corrie sought to amend the British 1967 Abortion Act to restrict the grounds on which women could get an abortion. The 1967 act had been a major victory for women's rights, and the 1979 campaign drew in wide forces, particularly from the trade union movement. Socialist Jan Neilsen remembers how the movement changed with the involvement of the organised working class when the Trades Union Congress (TUC) called an abortion rights protest in October 1979. The march was led by Len Murray, TUC general secretary:

> On the day of the TUC march itself it was, how can I say, it was a very, very different feel to other

> demonstrations. Firstly, my memory is that the march was at least 40 percent men. We had always had the odd dribble of men, socialist men, supporting NAC (National Abortion Campaign), but to have men carrying all your very traditional trade union banners on that demonstration—we knew that we had crossed the Rubicon. We knew that we had gone into a totally different political period and I can't tell you how elated we all felt to see Len Murray leading the demonstration. We didn't have any illusions about him but that was such an important step to have the TUC general secretary leading a demonstration to defend abortion rights.[349]

The Corrie Bill, as it became known, was eventually dropped.

Examples like this, together with those in the earlier accounts of revolutions, show that class struggle is an enormous teacher. In the process of struggle, workers learn a great deal about themselves, their bosses, the police and the system itself. Capitalism divides us from each other, using racism, sexism, homophobia and transphobia to make us think that the problem in society is not the bosses or the system, but refugees, migrants, other genders or the LGBT+ community. Marx wrote about this when discussing the way 19th century British capitalism used anti-Irish racism to divide workers. A divided workforce was one that was less able to unite together against the bosses.

> Every industrial and commercial centre in England now possesses a working class divided into two hostile camps, English proletarians and Irish proletarians. The ordinary English worker hates the Irish worker as a competitor who lowers his standard of life. In relation to the Irish worker he regards himself as a member of the ruling nation and consequently he becomes a tool of the English aristocrats and capitalists against Ireland, thus strengthening their domination over himself. He cherishes religious, social, and national prejudices

> against the Irish worker. His attitude towards him is much the same as that of the 'poor whites' to the Negroes in the former slave states of the USA. The Irishman pays him back with interest in his own money. He sees in the English worker both the accomplice and the stupid tool of the English rulers in Ireland.
>
> This antagonism is artificially kept alive and intensified by the press, the pulpit, the comic papers, in short, by all the means at the disposal of the ruling classes. This antagonism is the secret of the impotence of the English working class, despite its organisation. It is the secret by which the capitalist class maintains its power. And the latter is quite aware of this.[350]

But when workers stand together and fight, these divisions are challenged. Standing on a picket line with other workers, of different genders and nationalities, helps break down the prejudices that the capitalist system puts into people's heads. In the earlier account of the Sudanese revolution, we have seen how the government used racism towards people from Darfur as a way to divide the workers movement, and how the revolutionaries challenged this. The Russian Revolution took place in a country dominated by appalling misogyny and racism, yet women and Jewish people played leading roles in the revolution, and the revolution itself placed questions of racism and national oppression at the forefront of its programme.

This is not to say that there is no point challenging racism, sexism or other forms of oppression because the "class struggle will fix it". Indeed revolutionaries must be the "tribunes of the oppressed" standing up against oppression wherever it raises its head.

But the changes that take place in a revolutionary struggle transform people's ideas and attitudes on an enormous scale. Recall Peter Fryer's account of workers' councils during the Hungarian uprising of 1956, where he saw ordinary people, who had previously been "submerged" by the oppressive state capitalist system, transformed: "The revolution thrust them forward, aroused their civic pride and latent genius for organisation, set them to work to build democracy out of the ruins of bureaucracy".[351]

In 1848-1849 a wave of revolutions swept Europe. These were primarily bourgeois revolutions against the monarchy, for democracy and liberalism. Writing about events in France, Marx argued that the struggle transformed people very quickly indeed:

> In this torment of historical unrest, in this dramatic ebb and flow of revolutionary passions, hopes and disappointments, the different classes of French society had to count their epochs of development in weeks where they had previously counted them in half centuries. A considerable part of the peasants and of the provinces were revolutionised.[352]

Marx repeatedly emphasised that working people would be transformed by:

> A revolution, in which, on the one hand, the power of the earlier mode of production and intercourse and social organisation is overthrown, and, on the other hand, there develops the universal character and the energy of the proletariat, without which the revolution cannot be accomplished; and in which, further, the proletariat rids itself of everything that still clings to it from its previous position in society.[353]

Crucially, during struggle workers begin to learn their own power. Even the smallest strike can raise issues of organisation. But as strikes grow, or involve whole areas, they raise wider issues about control of the economy. In February 1919 the working class of Seattle went on strike and "took control of the city". The city authorities could do nothing, everything was in the hands of the workers. In his history of the strike Cal Winslow explains what happened:

> Rank-and-file workers, union by union, elected the strike leadership, a strike committee. The strike committee elected an executive committee. Meeting virtually nonstop, they ensured the health, welfare and safety of the city. Garbage was collected, the hospitals were supplied, babies got milk and the people were fed, including some thirty thousand a day at the strikers' kitchens.[354]

Throughout the history of capitalism, there have been countless examples like this from workers' struggles. They demonstrate that workers' have the power to organise society in a completely different way to the priorities of capitalism. They also show how, by going through a revolution, ordinary workers transform themselves. Marx and Engels famously wrote about the importance of this process:

> Both for the production on a mass scale of this communist consciousness, and for the success of the cause itself, the alteration of men on a mass scale is, necessary, an alteration which can only take place in a practical movement, a revolution; this revolution is necessary, therefore, not only because the ruling class cannot be overthrown in any other way, but also because the class overthrowing it can only in a revolution succeed in ridding itself of all the muck of ages and become fitted to found society anew.[355]

In making a revolution, workers throw off the "muck of ages"—their old racist, sexist, homophobic and transphobic ideas—but they also cast off all the old ruling class ideas that have held them back. These ideas, where workers are told they are not fit to govern, or are too stupid to organise their own workplaces, or need bosses to tell them how to work, are proved wrong by the experience of revolution. By going through a revolution, workers gain the collective outlook, the "communist consciousness" that enables them to build a new society completely different to capitalism. This is why Marx and Engels insisted that the emancipation of the working class must be the act of the working class itself—because that transformation cannot happen from outside, it must come out of workers' self-activity. Revolution is then, at its most simple, the self-emancipation of the working class.

*

The transformative possibility of struggle is one reason that socialists place such emphasis on workers' strikes. The other is that movements can develop far beyond their initial aims. The Paris Commune arose out of the discontent and poverty caused by war. The Russian revolution began in the context of war, food shortages and economic crisis and the revolutions in Egypt and Sudan arose out of opposition to the policies of hated dictators.

Such mass movements can then feed and encourage each other, allowing participants to generalise from their specific issues to wider questions and learn from different tactics about how to win, or move forward. The process is most obvious during mass strikes, as the Polish-German revolutionary Rosa Luxemburg explored in her book *The Mass Strike* written about the experience of the 1905 Russian Revolution:

> Every new onset and every fresh victory of the political struggle is transformed into a powerful impetus for the economic struggle, extending at the same time its external possibilities and intensifying the inner urge of the workers to better their position and their desire to struggle. After every foaming wave of political action a fructifying deposit remains behind

> from which a thousand stalks of economic struggle shoot forth. And conversely. The workers' condition of ceaseless economic struggle with the capitalists keeps their fighting energy alive in every political interval; it forms, so to speak, the permanent fresh reservoir of the strength of the proletarian classes, from which the political fight ever renews its strength.[356]

She continues, "The economic struggle is the transmitter from one political centre to another; the political struggle is the periodic fertilisation of the soil for the economic struggle".[357]

A protest movement can become a mass uprising, an uprising can develop into a revolutionary situation and a revolutionary situation can evolve into workers' power. But none of these steps are inevitable. Indeed most protests do not become uprisings, and revolutionary situations usually do not turn into situations of dual power. Whether they do or not depends on the specific situation and the conscious intervention of women and men arguing for the movements to take those steps.

In 1905 Soviets evolved out of the needs of the Russian workers' movement in that year of revolution. When similar organisations appeared again in 1917 it was in part because workers remembered them from the 1905 revolution, but also because they fitted the objective need for workers in revolution to coordinate, show solidarity and spread their movement. The absence of workers' councils in, say, the Egyptian revolution is not down to the failure of individuals; it is because the workers' movement did not reach the critical mass where these organisations fitted the needs of the movement. That is not to say there was no workers' organisation or coordination and it is certainly true that in Egypt in 2011 workers did organise themselves—to spread strikes, or protect their communities from Mubarak's forces. That such basic revolutionary organisation did arise shows that it might have developed further.

In these situations individuals can make an enormous difference—revolutionaries can call meetings, argue to spread struggle, or call for united action. Revolutionaries cannot conjure revolution from thin air, but they can act to develop the combativity and organisation of workers. The existence of organised revolutionaries can enable the workers' movement to take crucial steps forward, or navigate a changing political terrain.

Had the workers' revolts developed in Egypt and if there had been a mass revolutionary party of socialists pushing to develop workers' struggles and arguing for the coordination of strikes, sit-ins and protests, history could have been different. The building of such organisation—before revolution begins—remains a crucial task for socialists.

Of course, not every strike, campaign or mass movement develops into wider struggles. As each struggle unfolds, circumstances change, throwing up challenges for activists. Even in a revolutionary situation, there are ebbs and flows of struggle, quiet periods or times when reactionary forces are in ascendance. Think of how, as the Sudanese revolution unfolded, revolutionaries on the ground had to respond to the actions of the military. During the Russian revolution, the Bolsheviks had to navigate the challenges posed by the risings of the "July Days", government repression or the attempted far-right military coup led by General Kornilov. The challenge for the movement is always to draw on historical experience to develop the best way forward, the line of march that can strengthen the workers movement and the revolution in order to make it more likely to win.

At every stage of a revolutionary process there are different forces contesting the way forward. The ruling class will be trying to stop the revolution but at the same time there will be other forces, sometimes organised into political parties, that will want the movement to compromise or pause. They might argue that the movement is not ready, or that the revolution is premature, or going too far or be won over by promises of reforms or a share in power with the existing government. This is why it is crucial that there are also revolutionaries arguing for a way forward, drawing on past historical experience and an understanding of the power of the working class. If those revolutionaries are organised in a revolutionary party, they can maximise their impact. This was the role played by the Bolshevik Party in Russia in 1917. Such revolutionary organisation is crucial because, while class struggle is inevitable, its outcome is not.

During revolutions these questions are posed most sharply in conditions of dual power, when workers organisations—councils or soviets—are directly vying for power with the capitalist state. In such situations, the revolution can only go one of two directions. Either the working class will be defeated, or the workers themselves will seize power.

In normal times, only a minority of workers are convinced of the need for revolutionary change. In revolutions, the number of people who believe in their own power to transform society grows massively, and rapidly. Yet they are still bombarded with anti-revolutionary sentiments. This is why in the Egyptian and Sudanese revolutions, the ruling classes attempted to draw out the process of revolution, to sow doubt in the minds of the revolutionary classes, to undermine workers' confidence in themselves and their leaders. The presence of organised revolutionaries can help overcome these challenges, by using the networks that revolutionaries have developed, to move forward in a united way.

By grouping revolutionaries together in a political organisation, revolutionaries can maximise their ability to shape events and help move the revolution forward. They can draw on the historic experiences of the working class, as well as learn from the class itself. Lenin, during the Russian Revolution, was able to learn from the most militant sections of the working class in Petrograd, and generalise this across the Bolshevik Party as part of an argument that workers could seize power. At crucial moments, having such a network can help the revolution take major steps forward.

Even small revolutionary organisations can make a difference impact. As Naguib argues in his account of the

Egyptian Revolution of 2011, "Those of us in Tahrir Square during the uprising who believed that workers could finish off Mubarak didn't simply wait for strikes to happen. We went and argued with leading activists in the workplaces that workers could use their organised collective power against the regime".[358]

Small numbers of revolutionaries can make a difference. But a mass revolutionary organisation is needed if it is to relate to the hundreds of thousands, or millions of workers involved in a revolutionary movement. Had there been a revolutionary party of tens or hundreds of thousands in Egypt in 2011 it would have been able to develop the workers' struggle further, encouraging workers to take strike action and to build workplace organisations that might have taken on the organisation of the revolution itself, developing into networks of workers' councils. Had such councils existed there would have been an alternative to military rule of the generals and the bourgeois parliamentary democracy offered by Morsi. We have already seen how there is an urgent need for such a revolutionary party in Sudan.

Looking back at the historic examples discussed in this book, one event stands out: the Russian Revolution of 1917. This was the only time in history when workers took, and held, state power. The success of that revolution was due to the existence of the Bolshevik Party, an organisation whose members had been tested by struggles going back decades, which fought against oppression even under the difficult circumstances posed by Tsarist autocracy, and whose members were seen as respected leaders of the class. As a result, when the February revolution broke out, the Bolsheviks were able to grow massively throughout 1917, and ultimately lead the working class to victory. This has not yet been repeated, despite the heroism and bravery of revolutionaries in countless other revolutionary situations.

The "actuality of revolution" poses the question of revolutionary organisation. Building such an organisation is no easy task, yet the objective circumstances of the 21st century require it. The activity of such a revolutionary socialist party must be geared towards developing struggle. This must be contrasted to those who see socialism as being handed down from above, through the election of a left-wing government. The nature of the state makes this impossible and the capitalist system will block all but the most minor of reforms.

In the 21st century, a few reforms to capitalism will not be enough to avert climate catastrophe, prevent war and stop economic crisis. The alternative to socialist revolution will always be the violence, oppression and exploitation of capitalism. Socialists have to counterpose workers' power to the brutal reality of capitalism.

The introduction to this book quoted Rosa Luxemburg. During the slaughter of the First World War, she wrote that humanity faced a choice between "socialism or barbarism". Today the choice is even starker. Humanity faces the choice between socialism or extinction. It is a terrifying prospect. But in 1915 Luxemburg knew that the conditions of war and capitalism would lead to resistance and revolution. That remains true today. So Luxemburg concluded her *Junius Pamphlet* with a message of hope:

> This bloody nightmare of hell will not cease until the workers of Germany, of France, of Russia and of England will wake up out of their drunken sleep; will clasp each others' hands in brotherhood and will drown the bestial chorus of war agitators and the hoarse cry of capitalist hyenas with the might cry of labour, 'Proletarians of all countries, unite!'[359]

She was right to be optimistic. Workers' revolution ended the slaughter of that war, though it did not end capitalism. Today, avoiding the horrors of war and ecological destruction, and making sure humanity sees socialism, and not extinction, means completing that task.

Bibliography

Abidor, Mitchell, 2015, *Voices of the Paris Commune* (PM Press).

Alexander, Anne, 2019, "Living on revolution time: understanding the dynamics of the uprisings in Sudan and Algeria", *International Socialism* 163, Summer, p19-40. http://isj.org.uk/living-on-revolution-time/

Alexander, Anne, 2022, "All power to Sudan's resistance committees?", *SWP Long Reads*, 8 January. https://socialistworker.co.uk/long-reads/all-power-to-sudans-resistance-committees/

Alexander, Anne and Bassiouny, Mostafa, 2014, *Bread, Freedom, Social Justice: Workers & the Egyptian Revolution* (Zed)

Alneel, Muzan & Abdelrahman, Mohamed, 2022, "Interview: prospects for revolutionaries in Sudan", *International Socialism* 174, Spring, p66-80, www.isj.org.uk/interview-revolutionaries-in-sudan/

American Lung Association,2021, *State of the Air 2021*, ALA, www.lung.org

Angus, Ian, 2016, *Facing the Anthropocene* (Monthly Review Press)

Aronoff, Kate, 2021, *Overheated: How Capitalism Broke the Planet and How We Fight Back* (Bold Type Books)

Assaf, Simon, 2011, "Mubarak: ally of imperialism", *Socialist Review*, March. https://socialistworker.co.uk/socialist-review-archive/mubarak-ally-imperialism/

Barker, Colin, 1987, *Revolutionary Rehearsals* (Bookmarks)

Barker, Colin, Dale, Gareth & Davidson, Neil (eds), 2021, *Revolutionary Rehearsals in the Neoliberal Age* (Haymarket)

Beckett, Ben, 2019, *What Bernie Sanders and His Supporters Can Learn from Salvador Allende, Jacobin*, April. https://jacobinmag.com/2019/04/salvador-allende-chile-democratic-socialist-bernie

Berridge, Willow, Lynch, Justin, Makawi, Raga & de Waal, Alex, 2022, *Sudan's Unfinished Democracy: The Promise and Betrayal of a People's Revolution* (Hurst)

Bivar, Venus, 2018, *Organic Resistance: The Struggle over Industrial Farming in Postwar France* (University of North Carolina Press)

Bond, Patrick, 2011, *Durban's Climate Gamble: Trading Carbon, Betting the Earth* (Unisa Press)

Bond, Patrick, 2012, *Politics of Climate Justice: Paralysis Above, Movement Below,* (University Kwazulu Natal Press)

BP, 2021, *BP plc Group results: Fourth quarter and full year 2021*, bp.com/content/dam/bp/business-sites/en/global/corporate/pdfs/investors/bp-fourth-quarter-2021-results.pdf

Brunkard, Joan, Namulanda, Gonza & Ratard, Raoult, 2008, *Hurricane Katrina Deaths, Louisiana, 2005,* (Disaster Medicine and Public Health Preparedness)

Buchanan, Larry, Bui, Quoctrung & Patel, Jugal K, 2020, "Black Lives Matter May Be the Largest Movement in U.S. History", *New York Times*, 3 July. www.nytimes.com/interactive/2020/07/03/us/george-floyd-protests-crowd-size.html

Callinicos, Alex, 2001, "Having your cake and eating it", *Historical Materialism*, Vol. 9, 2001, pp169-195

Callinicos, Alex, 2003, *An Anti-Capitalism Manifesto* (Polity)

Callinicos, Alex, 2005, *Making History: Agency, Structure &*

Change in Social Theory (Haymarket)

Callinicos, Alex, 2006, "Alternatives to Neo-liberalism", *Socialist Review* 308, July

Carson, Rachel, 2000, *Silent Spring* (Penguin)

Canon, Gabrielle, 2021, "What the numbers tells us about a catastrophic year of wildfires", *Guardian*, 25 December. www.theguardian.com/us-news/2021/dec/25/what-the-numbers-tells-us-about-a-catastrophic-year-of-wildfires

Chase, Malcolm, 2021, *Early Trade Unionism* (Breviary Stuff Publications)

Chenoweth, Erica & Stephan, Maria, 2013, *Why Civil Resistance Works: The Strategic Logic of Nonviolent Conflict* (Columbia University Press)

Choonara, Joseph, 2020, "A new cycle of revolt", *International Socialism* 165, Winter, pp21-36. http://isj.org.uk/a-new-cycle-of-revolt/

Clement, Viviane, Kanta Kumari Rigaud, de Sherbinin, Alex, Jones, Bryan, Adamo, Susana, Schewe, Jacob, Sadiq, Nian & Shabahat, Elham, 2021, *Groundswell Part 2: Acting on Internal Climate Migration*, The World Bank

Cliff, Tony, 1988, *State Capitalism in Russia* (Bookmarks)

Cox, Judy, 2021, "Genderquake: socialist women and the Paris Commune", *International Socialism* 169, Winter. http://isj.org.uk/genderquake-paris-commune/

Crosby, Alfred W, 2010, *Ecological Imperialism: The Biological Expansion of Europe, 900-1900* (Cambridge University Press)

Devine, Pat, 2010, *Democracy and Economic Planning* (Polity)

Diffenbaugh, Noah S & Burke, Marshall, 2019, *Global warming has increased global economic inequality*, PNAS, 2019, p9808–9813. www.pnas.org/content/116/20/9808

Draper, Hal, 1977, *Karl Marx's Theory of Revolution: Volume I, State and Bureaucracy* (Monthly Review Press)

Draper, Hal, 1978, *Karl Marx's Theory of Revolution: Volume II, The Politics of Social Classes* (Monthly Review Press)

Draper, Hal, 1986, *Karl Marx's Theory of Revolution: Volume III, The "Dictatorship of the Proletariat"* (Monthly Review Press)

el-Hamalawy, Hossam, 2019, "Sudan at the crossroads", *Socialist Review*, May. https://socialistworker.co.uk/socialist-review-archive/sudan-crossroads/

el-Hamalawy, Hossam, 2021, "The Egyptian Revolution—18 days that shook the world", *Socialist Worker*, 18 January. https://socialistworker.co.uk/features/the-egyptian-revolution-18-days-that-shook-the-world/

Empson, Martin, 2014, *Land and Labour: Marxism, Ecology & Human History* (Bookmarks)

Empson, Martin, 2017, "Nature, Labor and the Rise of Capitalism", *Monthly Review* Vol 65, No 1, May 2017, https://monthlyreview.org/2017/05/01/nature-labor-and-the-rise-of-capitalism/

Empson, Martin, 2017, "A common treasury for all: Gerrard Winstanley's vision of utopia", *International Socialism* 154, Spring, http://isj.org.uk/a-common-treasury-for-all/

Empson, Martin, 2018, *Kill all the Gentlemen: Class Struggle and Change in the English Countryside* (Bookmarks)

Empson, Martin, 2020, "Non-violence, social change and revolution", *International Socialism,* Winter, http://isj.org.uk/non-violence-social-change-and-revolution/

Empson, Martin, 2021, *The Great Climate COP Out: Why COP26 will not solve the environmental crisis* (Socialist Worker)

Empson, Martin, 2022, "How can we stop capitalism's climate cop-outs?" *SWP Long Reads,* 15

January, https://socialistworker.co.uk/long-reads/how-can-we-stop-capitalisms-climate-change-cop-outs/

FAO, 2019, "The State of the World's Biodiversity for Food and Agriculture", J. Bélanger & D. Pilling (eds), FAO Commission on Genetic Resources for Food and Agriculture Assessments. Rome. 572 http://www.fao.org/3/CA3129EN/CA3129EN.pdf

Farrell, Clare and others (eds), 2019, *This Is Not A Drill: An Extinction Rebellion Handbook* (Penguin)

Feedback, 2018, *Farmers talk food waste: supermarkets' role in crop waste on UK farms*, Feedback. https://feedbackglobal.org/research/farmers-talk-food-waste-supermarkets-role-in-crop-waste-on-uk-farms/

Flannery, Kent & Marcus, Joyce, 2012, *The Creation of Inequality* (Harvard University Press)

Foster, John Bellamy & Clark, Brett, 2012, "The Planetary Emergency", *Monthly Review*, Vol 64, No 7, December

Foster, John Bellamy, 2020a, *The Robbery of Nature: Capitalism and the Ecological Rift*, (Monthly Review Press)

Foster, John Bellamy, 2020b *The Return of Nature: Socialism and Ecology* (Monthly Review Press)

Fryer, Peter, 1986, *Hungarian Tragedy* (New Park)

Gammage, Bill, 2012, *The Biggest Estate on Earth: How Aborigines made Australia*, (Allen & Unwin)

Gluckstein, Donny, 2006, *The Paris Commune: A Revolution in Democracy* (Bookmarks)

Geisler, Charles & Ben Currens, 2017, "Impediments to inland resettlement under conditions of accelerated sea level rise", *Land Use Policy* 66, p322-330

Habtezion, Senay, 2013, *Gender and Disaster Risk Reduction*, United Nations Development Programme

Hardy, Jane, 2021, *Nothing to lose but our chains: Work & resistance in 21st century Britain* (Pluto)

Harman, Chris, 1967, *Russia: How the Revolution was Lost, International Socialism* first series, No. 30. www.marxists.org/archive/harman/1967/xx/revlost.htm

Harman, Chris, 1988, *Class Struggles in Eastern Europe 1945-1983*, (Bookmarks)

Harman, Chris, 1989, "The Myth of Market Socialism", *International Socialism*, 42, Spring, pp3-62. www.marxists.org/archive/harman/1989/xx/marketsoc.html

Harman, Chris, 1991, "The state and capitalism today", *International Socialism* 51, Summer, pp3-54. www.marxists.org/archive/harman/1991/xx/statcap.htm

Harman, Chris, 1994, "Engels and the Origins of Human Society", *International Socialism* 65, Winter, pp83-142. www.marxists.org/archive/harman/1994/xx/engels.htm

Harman, Chris, 1999, *A People's History of the World* (Bookmarks)

Harman, Chris, 2007, *Revolution in the 21st Century* (Bookmarks)

Intergovernmental Panel on Climate Change (IPCC), 2022, *Impacts, Adaptation and Vulnerability: Summary for Policymakers*, UNEP, 2022

Intergovernmental Science-Policy Platform on Biodiversity and Ecosystem Services (IPBES), 2019, *Global assessment report on biodiversity and ecosystem services of the Intergovernmental Science-Policy Platform on Biodiversity and Ecosystem Services: Summary for policymakers*, IPBES secretariat

Jackson, Pete, 2012, *Close the Gates: The 1972 Miners' Strike, Saltley Gate and the Defeat of the Tories* (Bookmarks)

Jeffery, Suzanne (ed), 2021, *Climate Jobs: Building a workforce for the climate emergency* (Campaign Against Climate Change)

Kidron, Michael, 1974, *Capitalism & Theory* (Pluto Press)

Kimber, Charlie, 2019a, "Sudan sit-in shows how ordinary people can run society and win real change", *Socialist Worker*, 14 April. https://socialistworker.co.uk/international/sudan-sit-in-shows-how-ordinary-people-can-run-society-and-win-real-change/

Kimber, Charlie, 2019b, "Sudanese union calls general strike for 'full victory' against military", *Socialist Worker*, 28 May. https://socialistworker.co.uk/international/sudanese-union-calls-general-strike-for-full-victory-against-military/

Kimber, Charlie, 2019c, "Sudanese workers deepen revolt with a general strike against the regime", *Socialist Worker*, 11 June. https://socialistworker.co.uk/international/sudanese-workers-deepen-revolt-with-a-general-strike-against-the-regime/

Kimber, Charlie, 2019d, "Halt of general strike risks stalling the revolt in Sudan", *Socialist Worker*, 14 June. https://socialistworker.co.uk/international/halt-of-general-strike-risks-stalling-the-revolt-in-sudan/

Kimber, Charlie, 2019e "Rotten deal puts Sudan revolt at risk", *Socialist Worker*, 6 August 6. https://socialistworker.co.uk/international/rotten-deal-puts-sudan-revolt-at-risk/

Klein, Naomi, 2014, *This Changes Everything: Capitalism versus the Climate* (Allen Lane)

Klein, Naomi, 2019, *On Fire: The Burning Case for a Green New Deal* (Allen Lane)

Kovel, Joel, 2007, *The Enemy of Nature* (Zed Books)

Krantz, Mark, 2014, *The 1842 General Strike: Richard Pilling and the Lancashire Chartists* (Bookmarks)

Leather, Amy, 2021, *Capitalism and the Politics of Food* (Socialist Worker)

Lenin, V I, 1911, "In Memory of the Commune", *Rabochaya Gazeta*, No. 4–5, 15 April (28). www.marxists.org/archive/lenin/works/1911/apr/15.htm

Lenin, V I, 1915, "The Collapse of the Second International", *Kommunist* No. 1–2. www.marxists.org/archive/lenin/works/1915/csi/ii.htm#v21pp74h-212

Lenin, V I, 1917a, "The Tasks of the Proletariat in Our Revolution", September. www.marxists.org/archive/lenin/works/1917/tasks/index.htm

Lenin, V I, 1917b, "Can the Bolsheviks Retain State Power?", October. marxists.org/archive/lenin/works/1917/oct/01.htm

Lenin, V I, 1917c, "Meeting Of The All-Russia Central Executive Committee", 17 November. www.marxists.org/archive/lenin/works/1917/nov/04a.htm

Lenin, V I, 1992, *The State and Revolution* (Penguin)

Lissagaray, Prosper-Olivier, 1976, *History of the Paris Commune,* (New Press)

Lukács, Georg, 2009, *Lenin: A Study on the Unity of His Thought* (Verso)

Luxemburg, Rosa, 1900, *Reform or Revolution,* https://www.marxists.org/archive/luxemburg/1900/reform-revolution/

Luxemburg, Rosa, 1915, *The Junius Pamphlet,* www.marxists.org/archive/luxemburg/1915/junius

Maguire, Kevin, 2003, "Anti-war train drivers refuse to move arms freight", The Guardian, 9 January. www.theguardian.com/uk/2003/jan/09/politics.military

Malm, Andreas, 2016, *Fossil Capital* (Verso)

Malm, Andreas, 2021, *How to Blow Up a Pipeline* (Verso)

Malm, Andreas & the Zetkin Collective, 2021, *White Skin, Black Fuel* (Verso)

Mann, Michael E, 2021, *The New Climate War* (Scribe)

Marriott, James & Macalister, Terry, 2021, *Crude Britannia: How Oil Shaped a Nation* (Pluto Press)

Marx, Karl, 1934, *Selected Correspondence* (Lawrence & Wishart)

Marx, Karl, 1875, *Critique of the Gotha Programme*, www.marxists.org/archive/marx/works/1875/gotha/ch01.htm

Marx, Karl, 1973, *Grundrisse* (Penguin)

Marx, Karl, 1990, *Capital: Volume One* (Penguin)

Marx, Karl, 1981, *Capital: Volume Three*, (Penguin)

Marx, Karl & Friedrich Engels, *Manifesto of the Communist Party*, 1848 online at www.marxists.org/archive/marx/works/1848/communist-manifesto

Marx, Karl & Engels, Friedrich, 1991, *Selected Works*, (Lawrence and Wishart)

Marx, Karl & Engels, Friedrich, 2007, *The German Ideology*, (Lawrence and Wishart)

Masri, Shahir, Scaduto, Erica, Jin, Yufang & Wu, Jun, 2012 "Disproportionate Impacts of Wildfires among Elderly and Low-Income Communities in California from 2000–2020", International Journal of Environmental Research and Public Health, 2021 doi.org/10.3390/ijerph18083921

Merriman, John, 2014, *Massacre: The Life and Death of the Paris Commune of 1871* (Yale University press)

Morozov, Evgeny, 2019, "Digital Socialism? The Calculation debate in the age of big data", *New Left Review*, March/June, p33-67

Murphy, Kevin, 2007, *Revolution and Counterrevolution: Class Struggle in a Moscow Metal Factory* (Haymarket)

Naguib, Sameh, 2011, *The Egyptian Revolution* (Bookmarks)

Nature, 2021, "Sustainability at the crossroads", *Nature 600*, p569-570, 20 December. www.nature.com/articles/d41586-021-03781-z

Neale, Jonathan, 2014, *One Million Climate Jobs (4th edition)*, (Campaign Against Climate Change)

Newsinger, John, 2012, *Fighting Back: The American Working Class in the 1930s*, (Bookmarks)

Nevins, Allan and others, 1960, *Energy and Man: A Symposium* (Appleton-Century-Crofts)

Orr, Judith, 2011, "Egypt in revolt—Judith Orr's Cairo diary", *Socialist Worker*, 30 January. https://socialistworker.co.uk/features/egypt-in-revolt-judith-orr-s-cairo-diary/

Orr, Judith, 2017, *Abortion Wars; The fight for Reproductive Rights* (Policy)

Pilling, David, 2019, "Sudan's protests feel like a trip back to revolutionary Russia", *Financial Times*, 24 April. www.ft.com/content/3b84079a-6684-11e9-a79d-04f350474d62

Rappel, Ian, 2018, "Natural capital: a neoliberal response to species extinction", *International Socialism* 160, Autumn, p59-76. http://isj.org.uk/natural-capital/

Richards, John F, 2014, *The World Hunt: An environmental history of the commodification of animals* (University of California Press)

Rostami-Povey, Elaheh, 2010, *Iran's Influence* (Zed Books)

Roth, Andrew, 2021, "'Everything is on fire': Siberia hit by unprecedented burning", *Guardian*, 20 July. www.theguardian.com/world/2021/jul/20/everything-is-on-fire-siberia-hit-by-unprecedented-burning

Royle, Camilla, 2021, "Migration in an era of climate catastrophe", *International Socialism* 169, Winter, p53-76. http://isj.org.uk/migration-climate-catastrophe/

Sader, Emir, 2011, *The New Mole: Paths of the Latin American left* (Verso)

Salel, Heba, 2022, "Egypt asks for IMF support to help it weather Ukraine crisis", *Financial Times*, 23 March. www.ft.com/content/8d91db0f-8b8d-4184-b81f-0adca85ca692

Saleh, Heba and Terazono, Emiko, 2022, "Ukraine war sparks food shortages in Arab nations as wheat prices soar", *Financial Times*, 21 March. www.ft.com/content/b76d3414-4f11-4e46-9271-9309c06237df

Saltmarsh, Chris, 2021, *Burnt: Fighting for climate justice* (Pluto)

Saros, Daniel E, 2014, *Information Technology and Socialist Construction: The End of Capital and the Transition to Socialism* (Routledge)

Schlotterbeck, Marian, 2020, "Salvador Allende's Brief Experiment in Radical Democracy in Chile Began 50 Years Ago Today", *Jacobin*, 9 April. https://jacobinmag.com/2020/09/salvador-allende-chile-coup-pinochet

Sharp, Buchanan, 2010, *In Contempt of All Authority: Rural Artisans and Riot in the West of England, 1586-1660* (Breviary Stuff Publications)

Sherry, Dave, 2017, *Russia 1917: Workers' Revolution and the Festival of the Oppressed* (Bookmarks)

Smith, S A, 2017, *Russia in Revolution: An Empire in Crisis, 1890 to 1928* (Oxford University Press)

Sparrow, Jeff, 2021, *Crimes Against Nature: Capitalism & Global Heating* (Scribe)

Tengely-Evans, Tomáš, 2022, *The Shadow of Stalin* (Socialist Worker)

Thacker, Paul, 2021, "In Their Own Words: The Dirty Dozen Documents of Big Oil's Secret Climate Knowledge", *DeSmog*, 29 October. www.desmog.com/2021/10/29/

dirty-dozen-documents-big-oil-secret-climate-knowledge-part-1/

Trotsky, Leon, 1992, *The History of the Russian Revolution* (Pathfinder)

United Nations Environment Programme (UNEP), 2022, "Spreading like Wildfire—The Rising Threat of Extraordinary Landscape Fires", UNEP Rapid Response

Assessment. www.unep.org/resources/report/spreading-wildfire-rising-threat-extraordinary-landscape-fires

Vaughan, Adam, 2022, "We have 48% chance of breaching 1.5°C target by 2026, says Met Office", *New Scientist*, 10 May. www.newscientist.com/article/2319222-we-have-48-chance-of-breaching-1-5c-target-by-2026-says-met-office/

Weiner, Douglas R, 2000, *Models of Nature: Ecology, Conservation & Cultural Revolution in Soviet Russia* (University of Pittsburgh Press)

Wilson, Tom, 2021, "Shell pulls out of Cambo oil project in UK's North Sea", *Financial Times*, 2 December, www.ft.com/content/8dd5e6d2-602a-4fcc-8cc2-2db6845b500d

Winslow, Cal, 2020, *Radical Seattle: The General Strike of 1919* (Monthly Review)

Winstanley, Gerrard, 1973, *The Law of Freedom and Other Writings* (Pelican)

Wise, Timothy A, 2019, *Eating Tomorrow* (New Press)

Wolmar, Christian, 2010, *Engines of War* (Atlantic Books)

Zinn, Howard, 1995, *A People's History of the United States* (Harper Perennial)

Žmolek, Michael Andrew, 2014, *Rethinking the Industrial Revolution* (Haymarket)

Notes

Introduction

1 Nature, 2021.
2 Vaughan, 2022.
3 See Callinicos, 2003, p21-35 for a discussion of such "superficial critique[s]" of capitalism within the anti-globalisation movement.
4 An excellent background to the neoliberal economic policies in the context of the environmental crisis can be found in Aronoff, 2021, p110-120.
5 For more on the limitations of these strategies see Rappel, 2018 and Empson, 2021.
6 Klein, 2019, p90.
7 See the discussion in Callinicos, 2003, p76-80.
8 Harman, 2007, p13-14.
9 Choonara, 2020.
10 IPCC, 2022, p11
11 Luxemburg, 1915, Ch1.

Chapter 1: How capitalism is destroying the world

12 See www.ncdc.noaa.gov/sotc/fire/202113
13 Roth, 2021.
14 www.cbc.ca/news/canada/british-columbia/bc-heat-dome-sudden-deaths-revised-2021-1.6232758
15 Canon, 2021.
16 UNEP, 2022, p6
17 UNEP, 2002, p57
18 UNEP, 2002, p60
19 Habtezion, 2013, p1.
20 Habtezion, 2013, p3.
21 IPCC, 2022, p12
22 Brunkard and others, 2008, p1.
23 ALA, 2021, p25.
24 Masri and others, 2021.
25 Diffenbaugh & Burke, 2019, p9809-9810.
26 http://news.bbc.co.uk/1/hi/sci/tech/6532323.stm
27 www.carbonbrief.org/analysis-which-countries-are-historically-responsible-for-climate-change/
28 https://ourworldindata.org/contributed-most-global-co2
29 www.theguardian.com/uk-news/2019/oct/21/britain-is-g7s-biggest-net-importer-of-co2-emissions-percapita-says-ons
30 Figures quoted in Royle, 2021.
31 Royle, 2021.
32 www.unhcr.org/uk/news/latest/2016/11/581f52dc4/frequently-asked-questions-climate-change-disaster-displacement.html
33 Clement & others, 2021, pxxii.
34 Geisler & Currens, 2017, p322.
35 Geisler & Currens, 2017, p323.
36 Geisler & Currens, 2017, p329.
37 Royle, 2021.
38 IPBES, 2019, p24.
39 FAO, 2019, p114.
40 Leather, 2021.
41 Wise, 2019, p50.
42 IPBES, 2019, p26.
43 IPBES, 2019, p12.

Chapter 2: How capitalism works

44 IPBES, 2019, p25-26.
45 Marx & Engels, 1848, Chapter 1.
46 Callinicos, 2003, p36.
47 Marx, 1990, p741.
48 Marx, 1990, p742.
49 Kidron, 1974, p56.
50 https://lordslibrary.parliament.uk/food-waste-in-the-uk/
51 Feedback, 2018.
52 www.theade.co.uk/assets/docs/resources/Less_Waste_More_Growth_Report.pdf
53 Marx, Theories of Surplus Value, quoted in Harman, 1989, p14.
54 Quoted in Harman, 1989, p14.
55 See the discussion of this in Harman, 1989, p15-17.
56 Foster, 2020a, p221.
57 Readers who would like to explore the question of nature, value and human labour further are encouraged to see Foster, 2020a, p221-228.
58 Marx, 1973, p410.
59 Quoted in Gammage, 2012, p233.
60 Richards, 2014, p44.
61 I have explored this process further in Empson, 2017.

Chapter 3: Greening capitalism?

62 In this section, I will primarily look at the way the free market relates to carbon emissions. However, the commodification of nature is an approach used by capital to deal with

other environmental issues, such as the biodiversity crisis. See Rappel, 2018.

63 Lohmann, Larry, The Endless Algebra of Climate Markets, in Bond, 2011, p193.
64 Bond, 2012, p168-173.
65 IPCC, 2022, p19. Here the "high confidence" refers to the certainty with which the IPCC scientists draw these conclusions.
66 https://redd-monitor.org/2020/10/22/interview-with-larry-lohmann-the-corner-house-carbon-markets-do-not-need-to-be-fixed-they-need-to-be-eliminated
67 Klein, 2019, p87
68 Klein, 2019, p91
69 Klein, 2019, p26.
70 www.congress.gov/bill/116th-congress/house-resolution/109/text
71 Zinn, 1995, p383.
72 Newsinger, 2012, p74.
73 Quoted in Newsinger, 2012, p43.
74 Newsinger, 2012, p85.
75 Zinn, 1995, p384.
76 Saltmarsh, 2021, p86
77 Saltmarsh, 2021, p89
78 Saltmarsh, 2021, p99.
79 I have been part of the climate jobs campaign since its inception, and have been part of the editorial and writing teams that have produced the various editions of its report.
80 Jeffery, 2021, p3.
81 Jeffery, 2021, p7-8
82 Jeffery, 2021,p7.
83 Jeffery, 2021, p95-96.
84 Jeffery, 2021, p96.
85 Saltmarsh, 2021, p127.
86 Saltmarsh, 2021, p127-128.
87 Saltmarsh, 2021, p128.
88 Luxemburg, 1900, Ch8.

Chapter 4: Fossil fuel capitalism

89 www.statista.com/statistics/973337/largest-european-based-revenue/
90 www.ft.com/content/81696e63-38c5-4454-8a03-8a92fdc4ca5a
91 BP, 2022.
92 Žmolek, 2014, p415.
93 Marx, 1990, p617.
94 Marx, 1990, p168.
95 Marx, 1990, p497.
96 Marx, 1990, p497-498.
97 Marx, 1990, p498-499.
98 Marx, 1990, p499.
99 The historian Michael Žmolek demonstrates this in a discussion about the great Staffordshire pottery manufacturer Josiah Wedgwood noting that key to his success was not the adoption of machinery, but his reorganisation of labour and the manufacturing process, and crucially their subordination to a new labour discipline. Wedgewood can stand in for a capitalist class that understood that the exploitation of workers was fundamental to their profits, and machinery was subordinated to this goal. See Žmolek, 2014, p407-413.
100 Quoted in Malm, 2016, p124.
101 Malm, 2016, p155.
102 Malm, 2016, p152.
103 Marx, 1990, p908-911. I have written further on this in Empson, 2018, particularly chapter 7.
104 Marx, 1990, p915.
105 Žmolek, 2014, p413.
106 Empson, 2018, p219-227 & p229-249.
107 Žmolek, 2014, p456.
108 Sharp, 2010, p137-139. For background see Empson, 2018, p175-180.
109 Chase, 2012, p170.
110 Žmolek, 2014, p765.
111 See the accounts in Malm, 2016, p226-237. An excellent introduction to the general strike of 1842 is Krantz, 2014.
112 Quoted in Malm, 2016, p231.
113 Malm, 2016, p213-233.
114 Malm, 2016, p234.
115 Jackson, 2012, p10.
116 Jackson, 2012, p16.
117 Jackson, 2012, p20-21.
118 In August 2021, British PM Boris Johnson made a joke that Thatcher was an early advocate of a switch away from coal. It is worth being clear that Thatcher's decision to move the economy away from coal had nothing to do with the environment, and everything to do with defeating her working class opponents.
119 Rostami-Povey, 2010, p30.
120 Malm, 2016, p249-251. Malm also notes that between 1800 and 1870 the British population grew by 150 percent, compared to an increase in coal output of 720 percent. The climate crisis arose from the interests of capitalism, not the growth in population. See Malm, 2016, p255-257.
121 Malm, 2016, p253.
122 Angus, 2016, p129-130. See also Malm, 2016, p253.

123 Wolmar, 2010, p13 and p18.
124 Angus, 2016,p131.
125 Malm & Zetkin, 2021, p345-p346.
126 Malm & Zetkin, 2021, p349.
127 Crosby, 2009.
128 Malm & Zetkin, 2021, p352.
129 Angus, 2016, p131.
130 Angus, 2016, p147.
131 Bivar, 2018.
132 Empson, 2014, p167-169.
133 Marriott and Macalister, 2021, p99-102.
134 Carson, 2000, p39-41.
135 Marriott and Macalister, 2021, p102.
136 Nevins, Allan and others, 1960, p58. This and other documents relating to early oil company knowledge of global warming can be found online in Thacker, 2021.
137 Nevins, Allan and others, 1960, p70.
138 Sparrow, 2021, p96.
139 Mann, 2021, p25. Chapter 2 of Mann's book is an excellent history of the "Climate Wars".
140 Mann, 2021, p45.
141 Malm & Zetkin, 2021.

Chapter 5: The capitalist state

142 Marx and Engels, 1991, p552.
143 Draper, 1977, p251.
144 Draper, 1977, p244.
145 For more on pre-class societies and the emergence of class difference see Flannery & Marcus, 2012 as well as Harman, 1994 and specifically on the role of agriculture, see Empson, 2014.
146 Flannery & Marcus, 2012, p98.
147 Harman, 1994, p127.
148 Draper, 1977, p258.
149 Marx & Engels, 1848, Chapter I.
150 Draper, 1977, p259.
151 Harman, 1991, p13.
152 Saltmarsh, 2021, p124.
153 Saltmarsh, 2021, p125.
154 Saltmarsh, 2021, p127.
155 Beckett, 2019.
156 Barker, 1987, p42
157 Barker, 1987, p43.
158 Barker, 1987, p46.
159 Beckett, 2019.
160 Barker, 1978, p52.
161 Both quotes from Barker, 1987, p58.
162 Schlotterbeck, 2020.
163 Barker, 1987, p61.
164 Barker, 1987, p73.
165 Schlotterbeck, 2020.
166 Barker, 1987, p75.
167 Barker, 1987, p77
168 Sader, 2011, p81.
169 Sader, 2011, p82.

Chapter 6: Changing the world: What sort of movement do we need?

170 Some of this chapter is based on my article Non-violence, social change and revolution in International Socialism 165, Winter 2020. See Empson, 2020 that explores non-violent strategy in detail. For more on the 2019 revolts see Choonara, 2020.
171 2020's Black Lives Matter protests are likely to be the largest protest movement in human history, with estimates of between 15 and 26 million people in the US alone taking to the streets. See Buchanan & others, 2020.
172 Farrell, 2019, p100.
173 Here Hallam is referencing the work of Erica Chenoweth and Maria Stephan in their book Why Civil Resistance Works. See Chenoweth and Stephan, 2013.
174 Malm, 2021. Some of what follows is from an article I wrote in the aftermath of COP26, see Empson, 2022.
175 Malm, 2021, p28-29.
176 Malm, 2021, p67.
177 Empson, 2020.
178 Hardy, 2021, p33-34.
179 Hardy, 2021, p35.
180 Hardy, 2021, p39-40.
181 Hardy, 2021, p65.
182 Hardy, 2021, p54-55.
183 Choonara, 2020.
184 Marx & Engels, 1848, Ch1.
185 Hardy, 2021, p90-91.
186 Quoted in Callinicos, 2005, p175.
187 Callinicos, 2005, p176.
188 Maguire, 2003.
189 Malm, 2021, p69.
190 Klein, 2014.
191 Wilson, 2021.
192 Neale, 2014, p64.
193 Malm, 2021, p70.

Chapter 7: Revolutionary lessons

194 See Harman, 1999, p366-367 for a discussion of the Meiji Revolution and its implications.
195 Lissagaray, 1976, p3.
196 Marx & Engels, 1991, p278.
197 Gluckstein, 2006, p88-89.
198 Cox, 2021, p104.
199 Merriman, 2014, p75-76.

200 Abidor, 2015, p59.
201 Lenin, 1992, p39.
202 Gluckstein, 2005, p27.
203 Merriman, 2014, p67-68.
204 Merriman, 2014, p69.
205 Lissagaray, 1976, p241 and Merriman, 2014, p83.
206 Cox, 2021, p104.
207 Cox, 2021, p112.
208 Cox, 2021, p113.
209 Merriman, 2014, p80-81.
210 Quoted in Gluckstein, 2005, p32.
211 Gluckstein, 2005, p33.
212 Cox, 2021, p114.
213 Gluckstein, 2006, p158-161.
214 Marx, 1991, p274.
215 Marx, 1991, p275.
216 See Lissagaray, 1976, chapters 9 & 10.
217 Marx, 1991, p275.
218 Marx, 1991, p272.
219 Lissagaray, 1976, p267.
220 Lissagaray, 1976, p310 and Merriman, 2014, p250.
221 Lenin, 1911.
222 Abidor, 2015, p60.
223 In this section, I can only give a brief summary of Russia's revolutionary year and the aftermath. Two excellent introductions for those wanting to read more are Sherry, 2017 and Trotsky, 1992.
224 In this section I use the dates of the pre-revolutionary calendar in Russia, which was 13 days behind the calendar used in the West.
225 Murphy, 2007, p31-33.
226 Murphy, 2007, p35.
227 Sherry, 2017, p94.
228 Smith, 2017, p144.
229 Lenin, 1917a.
230 Smith, 2017, p143.
231 Quoted in Sherry, 2017, p208-209.
232 Draper, 1978, p170-174.
233 Quoted in Harman, 1999, p341.
234 Trotsky, 1992, p421-422.
235 Lenin, 1917c.
236 The best short account of the defeat of the Revolution is Harman, 1967. Tomáš Tengely-Evans' pamphlet is a good introduction to the rise of Stalinism, Tengely-Evans, 2022.
237 Murphy, 2007, p73.
238 Murphy, 2007, p83.
239 Tengely-Evans, 2022, p15.
240 Space prevents a detailed discussion of this, but Tony Cliff's work State Capitalism in Russia, remains the definitive explanation of how state capitalism developed and functioned. See Cliff, 1988.
241 Weiner, 2000, p13-14.
242 For a discussion on the exact translation, see Weiner, 2000, p ix.
243 Weiner, 2000, p20.
244 Weiner, 2000, p27.
245 Weiner, 2000, p29.
246 Quoted in Kovel, 2007, p225.
247 Assaf, 2011.
248 Barker & others, 2021, p274.
249 Barker & others, 2021, p273.
250 Barker & others, 2021, p275.
251 Alexander & Bassiouny, 2014, p113-115.
252 Barker & others, 2021, p276.
253 Barker & others, 2021, p274-275.
254 Shenker, 2016, p199.
255 Shenker, 2016, p200.
256 el-Hamalawy, 2021.
257 Naguib, Sameh in Barker and others, 2021, p277-278.
258 Orr, 2011.
259 Shenker, 2016, p224.
260 Naguib, 2011, p19.
261 Barker and others, 2021, p281-282.
262 Barker and others, 2021, p282.
263 Naguib, 2011, p27-28.
264 Barker and others, 2021, p284.
265 Barker and others, 2021, p285.
266 Barker and others, 2021, p286-287.
267 Barker and others, 2021, p289.
268 Barker and others, 2021, p292.
269 Barker and others, 2021, p296.
270 Barker and others, 2021, p297.
271 Barker and others, 2021, p299.
272 Barker and others, 2021, p304.
273 el-Hamalawy, 2021.
274 Salel, 2022.
275 Saleh & Terazono, 2022.
276 On women in the Sudanese Revolution see Berridge and others, 2022, p32, p86 & p179-185. On the specific question of women under the Bashir regime, see Alexander, 2019, p24.
277 Berridge & others, 2022, p181.
278 Berridge & others, 2022, p177.
279 Pilling, 2019.
280 Quoted in Kimber, 2019a.
281 Quoted in Berridge & others, 2022, p177.
282 Kimber, 2019b.
283 Berridge & others, 2022, p101.
284 Berridge & others, 2022, p93.
285 See Kimber, 2019c and Kimber, 2019d.
286 el-Hamalawy, 2019.
287 Kimber, 2019e.
288 Berridge & others, 2022, p124.

289 Berridge & others, 2022, p124.
290 Berridge & others, 2022, p211.
291 Berridge & others, 2022, p211.
292 Alexander, 2022.
293 Alneel & Abdelrahman, 2022, p70.
294 Alneel & Abdelrahman, 2022, p72.
295 Alneel & Abdelrahman, 2022, p79.
296 The "centre" refers to the area around Khartoum, which includes fertile agricultural land and the "periphery" which includes the plains supporting livestock farming and resources such as oil and gold.
297 Alexander, 2022.
298 Alneel & Abdelrahman, 2022, p77.

Chapter 8: The workers' state

299 Sherry, 2017, p151.
300 Lenin, 1917b.
301 Lenin, 1917b.
302 Lenin, 1992, p23.
303 The date is that of the old pre-revolutionary calendar, 13 days behind the Western calendar.
304 Quoted in Sherry, 2017, p158-159.
305 Draper, 1986, p269-270.
306 Draper, 1986, p270.
307 Draper, 1986, p273.
308 Lenin, 1992, p79.
309 Lenin, 1992, p80.
310 Lenin, 1992, p82.
311 Lenin, 1992, p23.
312 www.marxists.org/archive/marx/works/1877/anti-duhring/ch24.htm

Chapter 9: The socialist alternative to capitalism

313 I have explored Winstanley's radical vision in detail in Empson, 2017.
314 Lenin, 1992, p89
315 Marx and Engels, 1848, Chapter 2.
316 See Foster, 2020b, p141-142.
317 Foster, 2020b, p142.
318 Foster, 2020b, p145.
319 Foster, 2020b, p154.
320 Devine, 2010, p30.
321 Devine, 2010, p32.
322 Devine, 2010, p32.
323 Devine, 2010, p143.
324 What follows is a critique of the command economies that dominated Eastern Europe and the USSR until 1989 and 1991 respectively,+when those countries opened up their economies to neoliberal capitalism. It is worth pointing out the case of Cuba, which while a surviving state capitalist economy, has shown that even in the case of highly restrictive conditions imposed by the US's imperialist economic blockade central state direction of resources can solve short-term economic and social issues.
325 Devine, 2010, p59.
326 Devine, 2010, p63.
327 Harman, 1989, p7-8.
328 Callinicos, 2006.
329 Devine, 2010, p254-255.
330 Morozov, 2019, p61.
331 Morozov, 2019, p35.
332 Morozov, 2019, p62-63.
333 See a summary of Daniel Saros' ideas in Morozov, 2019, p63-65. Further detail in Saros, 2014.
334 Morozov, 2019, p56.
335 For more on the Hungarian revolution and other revolts against State Capitalism see Harman, 1988.
336 Fryer, 1986, p44-45.
337 Devine, 2010, p184.
338 See discussion in Devine, 2010, p168-170.
339 Marx, 1875.
340 Foster & Clark, 2012.
341 Quoted in Callinicos, 2001.
342 Marx, 1981, p959.

Chapter 10: The actuality of revolution

343 Lukács, 2009, p11.
344 Lukács, 2009, p12-13.
345 Lenin, 1915.
346 Marx, 1981, p959.
347 Draper, 1978, p28-30.
348 Draper, 1978, p31. See also Harman, 2007, p28-30.
349 Quoted in Orr, 2017, p164.
350 Marx, 1934, p289-290.
351 Fryer, 1986, p45..
352 Quoted in Draper, 1978, p77. Draper adds that "Struggle was the school in which the education took place; revolution speeded up the curriculum and enriched the course."
353 Marx & Engels, 2007, p93.
354 Winslow, 2020, p23-24.
355 Marx & Engels, 2007, p94-95.
356 Luxemburg, 2003, p[illegible]55
357 Luxemburg, 2003, p255.
358 Naguib, 2011, p43-44
359 Luxemburg, 1915, Ch8.